JESUS AND THE HOPE OF THE POOR

*LUISE SCHOTTROFF AND
WOLFGANG STEGEMANN*

**TRANSLATED FROM THE GERMAN
BY MATTHEW J. O'CONNELL**

WIPF & STOCK · Eugene, Oregon

Wipf and Stock Publishers
199 W 8th Ave, Suite 3
Eugene, OR 97401

Jesus and the Hope of the Poor
By Schottroff, Luise, and Stegemann, Wolfgang
Copyright©1986 Verlag Kohlhammer and Orbis Books
ISBN 13: 978-1-60608-858-6
Publication date 7/1/2009
Previously published by Orbis Books, 1986

Contents

Preface

This book originated in a realization that there is contradiction between the Bible and the interpretation of it by those of us involved in First-World churches and biblical scholarship. Without a doubt certain political experiences, especially those emerging from the Vietnam War, have contributed to our new sensitivity to this contradiction. The New Testament promises that the last shall be first and that the reign of God belongs to the poor. The First-World interpretative tradition says that the "poor" in those promises must be persons with whom we can identify. For example it might have us understand that the "poor" in the Bible merely signify those who are spiritually poor.

This book is also the result of a realization of how unjust it is to deprive the poor of their gospel by interpreting it in such a way that it becomes our promise, a promise to the wealthy.

The theology of liberation in a First-World context still has a long, hard road to go. In the years since this book was first published in German a certain amount of further work has been done by scholars who wish to articulate a First-World interpretation of the Old and New Testaments along the lines of liberation theology (see, e.g., Willy Schottroff and Wolfgang Stegemann, *The God of the Lowly* [Maryknoll, N.Y.: Orbis Books, 1984]). An investigation of the societal relationships, the "social context," of primitive Christianity is another important task awaiting Christians. Research in the area of social history has proved its worth in connection with liberation theology.

A further conviction has crystallized in the minds of the authors of this book: that it will be meaningful, indeed essential, always to take account of two contexts when studying the Bible. We reason from the following considerations. The Bible contains two contextual layers: its own and that of the individuals who read and interpret its pages. Now, neither of these two contexts will be available to biblical interpretation if that interpretation divorces faith from the everyday human situation in which economics, politics, and a military establishment determine, more often than not by raw force, the concrete human condition. This is the situation into which God's word entered and enters. It will not do to reduce the exemplary faith-situation to that of solitary believers praying in their chambers or on their deathbeds. The unemployed, too, roaming the streets, the starving children—yes, and the fond mother of a healthy baby, as she hopes and strives for her child's future—are, in their concrete situation, the subjects or agents of Christian faith. When we are speaking of faith we shall have to call political and social relationships by their right names.

This is the sort of biblical interpretation for which we ought to aim, whether the object of our research be our own situation or that of the men and women of biblical times.

This research must not be primarily the task of a specialized academic "elite." Perhaps the academicians will have to be called on for auxiliary tasks. But it will be the whole people of God who will be the actual interpreters of the Bible. Biblical interpretation is the concern of every Christian who would know the roots of his or her faith—who would know how the fathers and mothers of the faith have realized their hope in practice.

Research into our own situation today will strictly demand that we live in solidarity with others in the same situation, as well as in solidarity with "those beneath." An investigation of the historical situation of biblical times involves an analogous solidarity. For centuries, Western Europeans' interpretation of the Bible was anti-Semitic. Jesus appeared as the vanquisher of a legalistic, formalistic Jewish ideology and piety—as the one who brought a better gospel, a gospel that eclipsed all that preceded it. Only by taking "two steps forward and one backward," and with Auschwitz now a part of our experience, are we Christians finally beginning to move beyond our interpretative tradition and begin to grasp that what Jesus did was advance the history of the relation of God with God's people and with all humanity; Jesus did not void history.

For centuries, biblical interpretation was antifeminist. Women were either simply left out of account or else were seen in the role of the "ideal" woman, as the one who brings children into the world, patiently endures suffering, and is man's helpmate. Our Western European interpretative tradition has simply concealed the fact that women in the Bible have an altogether different role.

For centuries, our biblical interpretation has made the poor objects of our solicitude, and those texts which declare that the poor are "first" and that they are the ones to whom "the reign of God belongs" have been spiritualized—"lifted" to a symbolic level.

If we combine all of these observations into a prescription or recipe for reading the Bible, we obtain the following result:

1. Our habit of depriving the biblical texts of their concretion and spiritualizing them must be noticed and amended. When poverty is mentioned in the text, we must not read "poverty"—poverty in a merely symbolic sense.

2. Oppressed persons, the unemployed, Jews, women, children, the sick, and so on, must no longer be overlooked and tacitly or explicitly "disqualified" from being key figures in the biblical milieu.

3. The reality of human beings' lives must be grasped as concretely as possible. "Humankind" as an anthropological quantity, timeless and abstract, should no longer appear in biblical interpretation.

4. It is not necessary to read extra biblical texts in order to understand the Bible and its context. The Bible is in its own right a sociohistorical treasure-trove of the first order. Once we have read a whole Gospel from start to finish

using the approach sketched above, we shall be able to give a very precise description of the situation of women, workers, or the sick in the context of that Gospel, and we shall have a far more concrete conceptualization of what faith in the Risen One meant in the practical order for men and women of New Testament times. Supplementary sociohistorical information, from extrabiblical sources, will normally be accessible only to those who have the time and opportunity for historical research. They can assist the Bible-reader, but the latter will not be dependent on them.

5. The history of biblical faith and life will not yield its existential consequences for our situation today if we pigeonhole it in some abstract category that we happen to have learned about or conjectured. That history will acquire clarity and meaning only in proportion to the clarity of our grasp of the actual situation of living, breathing believers. We shall have to come to grips with our own and others' actual interests, in a context of the social, economic, and political presuppositions and options constituting our concrete reality. Theological discourse without this explicit, concrete attention to the situation and interests of those involved in the discourse conjures up a false, deceptive "neutrality." However, the existential consequences of a confrontation with the biblical tradition can never be nonpartisan. Living as I do in a wealthy, industrialized nation I can have a contemporary experience of the meaning of faith only if I realize that the wealth of my country is built on and perpetuated by the unjust exploitation of the raw materials and products of the Third World. In the absence of any effort to change this basic injustice of our existence, Christian faith will be inaccessible to us. God's "partiality," God's partisanship with the poor and oppressed, which is an essential aspect of God's universal salvific will, has immediate consequences for faith-in-action. The activity and the hopes of the believers of whom we read in the Bible are the activity and hopes of believers in particular, concrete situations. Any translation of the concrete faith-in-action of biblical times into our concrete situation today will require a recognition on our part of analogous relationships between biblical times and our own. The cogency of Ernesto Cardenal's *The Gospel in Solentiname* (Maryknoll, N.Y.: Orbis Books, 4 vols.) springs precisely from the fact that the peasants of Solentiname and the first Christians whose faith is expressed in the Gospels of the New Testament are linked by the similarity between the concrete situations that make up the context of their respective lives of faith. The historical gap of two millennia can easily be of less relevance than the social gap between the men and women of New Testament times and, for example, a white, middle-class elite in an industrialized country. The social gap can be bridged, however. We need only to start off down the road to "peace and justice" in the meaning those terms have in authentic biblical tradition. There, their meaning is partisan. The Bible "takes sides."

Our audience will note that while the reading of the Bible done in this book indeed follows the method sketched above, it also calls on scholarship. Historical criticism cannot simply be dispensed with. The biblical texts are the product of human history—a faith history, to be sure, but history nonetheless. Thus, diverging from the approach customarily taken in First-World academic circles, our criticism will take the sociohistorical perspective into account, which will of course preclude any shunting of the question of concrete, existential solidarity. Obviously social history can be done "from above," from an ivory tower, but our own scholarly hermeneutics will remain purely ancillary, as we suggested above.

The authority of the Bible is the authority of the living, breathing faith of human beings expressing themselves in its texts. From their testimony we experience Christ as the Liberator, the One who delivers people from the powers of death. And so a confrontation with the biblical tradition is a conversation with human beings who have lived the faith before us, in their own situation. Thus we may come near them—despite the historical, and often social, chasm that yawns between us—with a salutary curiosity. For when we take both contexts of the Bible seriously, it is then that—despite the historical and often the social gap—we are enabled to learn things from our fathers and mothers in faith that we can apply to our own praxis. We shall have to "translate the faith" from its biblical context into our own. Only one blind to the Bible's double context can turn it into a book of private faith and say that sacred scripture is of no use in dealing with contemporary social questions. Only those blind to the Bible's double context can proclaim that Jesus had nothing to say about nuclear war (see Luise and Willy Schottroff, *Die Parteilichkeit Gottes* [Munich: Kaiser, 1984], pp. 8–12).

LUISE SCHOTTROFF

Abbreviations Used

b	Babylonian Talmud (with tractate):
bBB	Baba Batra
bBK	Baba Kama
bNed	Nedarim
bSab	Sabbath
bSanh	Sanhedrin
bSota	Sota
bTaan	Taanith
Billerbeck	H. L. Strack and P. Billerbeck, *Kommentar zum Neuen Testament aus Talmud und Midrasch,* vols. 1–4 (Munich, 1922–28)
BK	Baba Kama (of Mishnah)
BZ	*Biblische Zeitschrift*
CIS	*Corpus Inscriptionum Semiticarum* (Paris, 1881ff.)
Dig.	Digest(s) of *Corpus iuris civilis*
EvTh	*Evangelische Theologie*
JAC	*Jahrbuch für Antike und Christentum*
JB	Jerusalem Bible
JTS	*Journal of Theological Studies*
Ned	Nedarim (of Mishnah)
NovTest	*Novum Testamentum*
par.	parallel(s)
Q	*Quelle* = Sayings-source
SBT	Studies in Biblical Theology
TDNT	*Theological Dictionary of the New Testament*
ZDMG	*Zeitschrift der deutschen morgenländischen Gesellschaft*
ZNTW	*Zeitschrift für die neutestamentliche Wissenschaft*
ZTK	*Zeitschrift für Theologie und Kirche*
//	indicates synoptic Gospel parallels

NOTE: Scripture passages are quoted from the Revised Standard Version of the Bible unless credited otherwise. Citations with a "Q" following are reconstructions of the text of the Sayings-source, made on the basis of Matthew and Luke parallels.

1

"The Poor Have Good News Preached to Them": The Earliest Tradition about Jesus of Nazareth

I. HISTORICAL JESUS OR EARLIEST TRADITION ABOUT JESUS? AN INTRODUCTION TO THIS BOOK

1. What Can Be Said about the Historical Jesus?

On the one hand, very little can be said about the historical Jesus, especially if we are looking for verbatim quotations (*verba ipsissima*) of what he said and for sure historical details. From the historical standpoint, the death of Jesus on the cross is the most certain and unambiguous fact reported about him. Even a skeptical historian will not doubt that Jesus, a Jew living in an Israel that was then under Roman rule, became the center of a religious movement and was eventually crucified by the Romans, probably at the instigation of certain powerful leaders of the Jewish people.

The death of Jesus, simply as a historical fact, is quite beyond doubt. The man was felt to be politically dangerous, and the cross was an instrument used by the Romans to ensure political discipline of the restless Jewish populace. Among those crucified were, for example, politically active individuals, prisoners of war, and refugees such as the ones who tried to escape from the besieged and starving city of Jerusalem.[1] Rudolf Bultmann has said that Jesus was crucified "because his activity was misconstrued as a political activity."[2] He put it this way because he assumed, and with justification, that the Jesus movement did not pursue explicitly political aims and activities. The statement is incorrect, however, to the extent that a movement such as that of the followers of Jesus could not but seem politically dangerous to the political leaders of the country. In that sense his death was not due to a misunderstanding.

Apart from his death by crucifixion hardly any details about the historical

1

Jesus can be claimed as historically certain. In particular, it is almost futile to attempt to prove the historical "authenticity" of any of the sayings of Jesus that are transmitted in the Gospel tradition. It is futile because the synoptic Gospels speak of the Jesus who is an object of faith, and not of the "historical" Jesus in the modern sense of the term.

On the one hand, then, it is hardly possible to ascertain any historically sure details regarding Jesus. On the other hand, it is possible to say a good deal that is historically reliable about Jesus provided we no longer isolate him from the individuals who first thought of themselves as his followers, that is, from his disciples both in his lifetime and in the period immediately following his death. If we attempt to understand him in the context of the earliest Jesus movement, we can draw a good many historically valid conclusions regarding him.

The historian, then, cannot isolate Jesus from his disciples. But then neither can the theologian afford to do so. The choice between an authentic, that is, historical Jesus, and an unauthentic Jesus who was the product of community thinking, determined Gospel research for a long time, and indeed we owe it some very important advances in that area. It should, however, cease any longer to determine our approach to the sources, and this even for theological reasons. The choice really represents an attempt to isolate Jesus, to set him apart from his disciples and remove him from Judaism so that he stands on the lonely pedestal of the inspired hero whose genius emerges all the more clearly, the more removed he is from the people among whom he lives.

In principle, however, Jesus is inseparable from certain groups among the Jewish people; above all, he is inseparable from his first disciples. He was one of those Jews who in the first half of the first century began to proclaim the reign of God in a unique and momentous way. For this reason, in contexts in which the concern is with historical fact it is better not to speak of the historical Jesus but, rather, of the earliest Jesus movement and—in dealing with the sources—of the earliest tradition about Jesus (the Jesus tradition). In theological contexts, on the other hand, we can confidently retain the shorthand term "Jesus."

Given this presupposition, what can we say about the historical Jesus? He was probably the originator of a collective movement of poor Jews who, if we examine their real situation, had few opportunities for a decent life and little chance of survival. Moreover, and probably from the beginning, Jesus did not simply proclaim the approaching reign of God but was himself a symbol of hope; he was both the proclaimer and the proclaimed. The historical Jesus and the Jesus of faith (the historical Jesus and the kerygmatic Christ) are inseparable. The sayings of Jesus in the earliest Jesus tradition are already at the same time sayings *about Jesus*. An example will explain what is meant. "Blessed are the poor" is a sentence that we find on the lips of Jesus and that describes his concern for the poor. At the same time, however, it says something about Jesus: the promise of Isaiah (61:1ff.) is fulfilled by the coming of Jesus. Thus the earliest Jesus tradition is also a Christological Jesus tradition.

2. The Historical and the Theological Tasks

a. MEANING AND POSSIBILITY OF HISTORICAL RECONSTRUCTION

Because portraits of Jesus—intended as portraits of the historical Jesus—have often varied according to the standpoint of the viewer, they have given rise to a kind of historical cynicism. One consequence of this attitude can be that people think it senseless and a waste of time to pay attention to the historical past. The current widespread disinterest in biblical scholarship in the church is certainly to some extent the fault also of biblical scholars themselves, but that is not the real problem. The real problem is that acquaintance with the biblical tradition is regarded as something secondary. Individuals may have certain humanitarian goals and later on find these to be already in the Bible; they may have a certain idea of the faith and seek to justify their corresponding religious interests from the Bible. In both cases, the Bible is assigned only a secondary role; in both cases individuals initially take only themselves seriously and then attempt to harness the Bible in the service of their concerns.

Defeatism in regard to historical work and to any meaning the content of Scripture might have for our time is wrong, rash, groundless and, in the final analysis, impious, since it means we no longer trust other human beings—those, for example, who were part of the earliest Jesus movement and from whose hopes we today could learn a lesson if only we would involve ourselves with them.

Just as we do our contemporaries the honor of taking them seriously and trying to understand them as accurately and concretely as possible, so too we should honor the people of the recent or distant past. Are we therefore saying that a scholarly knowledge of the Bible is needed in order to live today as a follower of Jesus? That would be absurd. We do assert, however, that the following of Jesus in our day is inseparable from listening to the words spoken about Jesus and his followers of long ago. This listening entails in turn a certain interest in history. How can anyone not want to know what it was really like in the past, once he or she realizes that the Gospels, for example, have something to tell us that we do not already know?

There is no denying, of course, that the present position or situation of interpreters influences their dialogue with history. On the other hand, interpretations cannot be multiplied at will, nor can the tradition be limitlessly manipulated in an arbitrary manner. The historical evidence for a given interpretation has also to be considered; all the more so, the more clearly the presuppositions that interpreters bring to their work are explicated.

b. COMING TO GRIPS WITH THE GOSPELS

Before we go any further, we must let the reader know the main stages by which we came to an understanding of the Gospels as documents that were produced by faith in Jesus and to which we do not do justice if we try to extract a "historical Jesus" from them. The explanation could, of course, have been found in Martin Kähler's book,[3] published in the United States in 1964; in all likelihood the reader did in fact find it, but did not accept it. Why? Because although in the "form-criticism" (*formgeschichtlich*) period of exegetical science, scholars considered it impossible to reconstruct the life of Jesus, some of the most reputable among them did not hesitate to regard certain sayings of Jesus as authentic. Along with Ernst Käsemann,[4] we thought the question of the historical Jesus a legitimate one and, from the theological point of view, even indispensable if we were to avoid succumbing to a *theologia gloriae* that regards the humanity of Jesus as unimportant.

But as the redaction-history approach to the Gospels began to produce results, it became increasingly clear that these documents were not formed from collections of sayings of the historical Jesus. They were, rather, portrayals of experiences that disciples had in their following of Christ at the various historical stages of early Christianity. The figures of the evangelists (Matthew, Mark, Luke) became increasingly well delineated; they were even "composers" of tradition about Jesus and were themselves responsible for some passages in their writings. The theological shape of the Sayings-source (Q) and the Christological implications of even the earliest Jesus tradition likewise became increasingly clear. As a result, the attempt to demonstrate "authenticity" turned into a struggle like that of Laocoön with the serpents, and in the process the content of the synoptic tradition was increasingly lost from sight.

Meanwhile, another factor was at work: we are learning to look upon Jesus as a human being in the midst of his fellows, as Jesus our brother. This new outlook helped us to regard Christian faith as an existential possibility for ourselves, far more so than when we had confessed Jesus as the distant God, the Messiah, the Son of God, to whom we had to look up and from whom we learned nothing but that a vast gulf existed between him and us. The gulf became especially clear when we reflected on the demands made of us in the Sermon on the Mount: the more divine Jesus is, the more impossible these demands become for us sinners.

Two presuppositions, then, led us to the approach to the Gospels that will be taken in this book. The first is the insight that in all their component parts the Gospels speak to us of the following of Jesus, and not of the historical Jesus in the modern sense of this term. The second is that Jesus, as symbol of Christian faith, as symbol of hope, is a human being among his fellows; he is a brother and not a metaphysical entity.

From the standpoint of method this means that we look upon the Gospels as a product of a historical Jesus movement. We move not from authentic parts to unauthentic, but from earlier parts to later. In dealing with individual texts, however, we find it advisable to move in the opposite direction: from the most recent stratum back to the earliest. We must ask ourselves, for example, What is the meaning of this or that word as found in Luke's Gospel? Can the word be traced back to earlier tradition? Is it possible to determine its literary and social context in that earlier tradition?

From the literary point of view, the most important stages in the Jesus movement that stands behind the Gospels can be lined up this way: a) The earliest Jesus tradition[5]; b) The Sayings-source (Q); c) The Gospel of Mark; d) The Gospel of Luke; e) The Gospel of Matthew. Not only do these represent five different theological outlines; they also reflect five distinct historical situations. It is likely that the picture could be nuanced even further, but these five are certainly the most important stages in the history of the Jesus movement. In opposition to ingrained ecclesiastical and, to some extent, scientific custom, we have already begun to read the Gospels as complete literary works; for example, to read the Gospel of Luke as a unified whole. The same principle applies to the earliest Jesus tradition and to the Sayings-source. By proceeding in this way we gain insight into the theological aim of the stratum or Gospel in question.

c. THE SOCIOHISTORICAL QUESTION

If we are to understand what it meant to follow Jesus in the various historical stages with which we shall be dealing, we must also know the world in which this following occurred. "World" here includes the religious context and the political situation, but also the social situation in the society under discussion.

When it comes to the comparative history of religions and the political order, we have admirable tools at our disposal. An adequate knowledge of the relevant social relationships, on the other hand, lies largely in the future. So many questions remain to be answered in this area that we can only hope that increasing numbers of scholars will cultivate an interest in the work. There is, of course, even here a tradition of research, which they can continue, although it dates primarily from the end of the nineteenth century and the beginning of the twentieth. The chief names to be mentioned are L. Friedländer and A. von Harnack.[6]

Among works of scholarship produced in recent decades those of Joachim Jeremias rank high.[7] Moreover, in addition to theology, other branches of study have likewise produced valuable tools; we may think, for example, of the historians of antiquity and the historians of jurisprudence. From the viewpoint of method, form criticism provides a point of departure. It must be noted, however, that when the older form critics raised the question of the "life context" (*Sitz im Leben*), they thought too narrowly in terms of religious and literary institutions (the liturgy as locus for the maintenance and development of tradition; etc.). The inquiry into the "life context" or "sociological context" must be extended to include the economic and social conditions of life.

The sociohistorical approach is not merely a way of making our picture of the past more colorful. Its real purpose is a theological one. The following of Jesus was a way of life that brought together human beings who were living lives of affliction. The affliction, then as now, was produced by repression, hatred, violence, and exploitation. Anyone who reduces the following of Jesus to an enterprise of the heart, the head, and private interpersonal relations restricts the following of Jesus and trivializes Jesus himself. Fernando Belo[8] provides us with a vivid image for the following of Christ. This following is, he says, a practice of the hands, the feet, and the eyes. The practice of the feet is brotherhood and gives expression to the political dimension of hope. A brother cannot bear to see other men and women in chains. The practice of the eyes is the capacity for criticism and the clarity of vision given by faith, which sees through the many lies told by the ideologies of power.

The authors of this book see it as a necessarily incomplete attempt to present in a more accurate way the sociohistorical dimension of the following of Jesus. No matter what the criticisms leveled against the book, our purpose will be fulfilled if those who complain about its defects do not limit themselves to complaints but make the sociohistorical task their own. This task makes its appearance as soon as the following of Jesus moves to the practical level. At that point one is grateful for information on how our brothers and sisters at the beginning of Christianity lived their concrete lives.

We offer this justification for our choice of questions: we focus our attention chiefly on texts that take a position on social problems, because in the earliest tradition, in the Sayings-source, and in the Gospel of Luke these texts occupy a central position in the material treated. In each case, of course, the tradition must be seen in light of the overall theological program. We are not aiming, however, at a complete presentation of any level (earliest tradition, Q, Luke).[9]

II. TAX COLLECTORS, SINNERS, PROSTITUTES, BEGGARS, THE POOR, AND CRIPPLES

Especially for the earliest Jesus tradition but also for its acceptance and continuation in the later stages of the following of Jesus (here: Q and Luke) it makes sense to gather together sociohistorical information on groups of persons who, as followers of Jesus, play an important role in the Jesus movement. Among these groups, tax collectors, sinners, prostitutes, beggars, the poor, and cripples call for special attention.

The necessity of getting as concrete a picture as possible of these social groups also becomes clear when we try to grasp fully the exegetical tradition that the authors are adopting here. If we consider the poor, whom Jesus calls blessed, to be poor in the economic sense of the word,[10] then it cannot be a matter of indifference to know what "poverty" meant in the world of Jesus' first disciples. Were these poor just a few beggars, peripheral figures in a population that, as far as the others went, were fairly well provided for? Or was poverty an affliction that beset a substantial part of the population? What are we to understand by "poverty"?

The familiarity of Jesus with tax collectors and prostitutes must also be represented with as much historical concreteness as possible before we can draw theological conclusions from the fact. At the time of which we are speaking, there is a widespread impression that tax collectors are well off and fraudulent people. They are scorned by the rest of the people for their cooperation with the Roman administration (therefore as collaborators) and because of their swindling. But the love of God now becomes a reality for these people in the words and deeds of Jesus.[11] No longer are these social outcasts condemned by God.[12] The Pharisees or even the Jewish populace generally criticize Jesus for consorting with tax collectors and sinners, "because he is doing what is God's prerogative."[13] H. Braun interprets the criticism of the Pharisees somewhat differently: they forbid Jesus to consort with tax collectors and sinners because in the Pharisees' eyes these people are religiously and morally beneath consideration.[14]

When we attempt to describe this situation in realistic terms, unanswered questions arise: How is Jesus regarded by his adversaries? Why is it that this simple man of the people evokes protests by his religious claims or, as the case may be, his scorn for religious and social (pre)judgments? Do his adversaries regard him as an important religious and social figure?

A second difficulty arises when we ask what precisely it means to be a tax collector. The problem latent here becomes visible especially when theological conclusions are drawn. Is the fate of the tax collectors to be compared to that of the Jews in the Third Reich[15] or are they, rather, "nonconformists' (H. Braun)? In what follows, our primary effort will be to gather historical information about the groups of people who became part of the Jesus movement.

1. Tax Collectors

Mark 2:15 tells us that Jesus and his disciples attended a banquet in the house of Levi the tax collector and that "many tax collectors and sinners" also took part. Even if the story in Mk. 2:13-17 is not in its entirety a historical report and if not all the details can be regarded as historically correct, the following presuppositions nonetheless are probably historically accurate: the Jesus movement was popular among tax collectors; there were many tax collectors in Palestine; the tax collectors in question were primarily people who sat in the tax offices (Mk. 2:14) and collected the *portatorium*;[16] the Jesus movement was criticized because of its openness to tax collectors.

The role played by "tax collectors" calls for nuanced treatment. As will be shown, we must distinguish from several points of view between tax farmers and their employees. And in the subsequent discussion of the problems raised by contempt for tax collectors there will likewise be need of nuancing, to the extent that the entire populace did not share the same (pre)judgments.

TAX FARMERS

In the first century A.D. Israel under Roman domination had more tax farmers and tax-office employees than did many other areas of the Roman empire. During this period the Romans in Palestine retained the already proven and profitable pre-Roman system of tax collection. Numerous small entrepreneurs from among the native population contracted with the Roman administration to collect the "taxes." At times similar contracts were made with cities that had kept the right to collect local taxes.

These businessmen had to pay their lease in advance and then try to make a profit in the course of the year for which their lease was good. Such a business was quite risky, as is already clear from the many stories of tax collectors being cheated,[17] and we may conclude that these men were subject to economic pressures. We must assume, in fact, that the situation revealed in the *Corpus iuris civilis* of Emperor Justinian (published beginning in A.D. 529) was paralleled in first-century Palestine: "If the eagerness of a bidder at the auction of taxes has inflated the offer beyond what is usually bid, the offer is to be accepted provided the winner in the bidding is prepared to give suitable guarantors and security . . . . Bidders who have not yet paid for their previous contract may not bid on a new one."[18]

Some tax farmers may have achieved prestige and wealth. Josephus tells of John, a Jewish tax collector at Caesarea, who became a leading man of the city. [19] Luke speaks of a rich "chief tax collector" named Zacchaeus in Jericho. And the Jewish legend of Ma'jan the tax collector, which has come down in several versions, tells of a tax collector who was well to do, although not respected by the distinguished folk of the city.[20] There is, however, no basis for the assumption that every tax farmer became rich. The not infrequent impression that all tax collectors were rich is due to Luke 19 or to scholars mistakenly identifying conditions in the Roman imperial age with those of the republic. As a matter of fact, the whole system of taxes and duties was organized quite differently in the republican period. There were associations for the collection of taxes; these had vast amounts of capital available and were so powerful that they became a political problem. The small tax farmers of the imperial age also had to have capital if they were to buy their leases; it was another question, however, whether the business would bring a profit, or not.

TAX EMPLOYEES

The tax farmers had the actual work of collection done by slaves and other employees. Luke shows a good grasp of the situation in Roman tax collecting when he distinguishes between "chief tax collector" and "tax collector," that is, a tax farmer and an everyday collector, probably a tax-office employee, subordinate collector, or the like.[21] In this matter, too, we may use the Digests of the *Corpus iuris civilis* to illustrate the situation.

The Digests assume that the *publicanus* (tax farmer) will employ his own slaves, but also "vagabond and runaway slaves" as well as free men who hire themselves out as slaves to the tax farmer (Dig. 39, 4, 12). The *telōnai* of the synoptic tradition, the men who actually sit in the customhouses (like Levi, in Mk. 2:14) are probably for the most part not the tax farmers but subordinates who deal with the public. If we assume that the same conditions held in first-century Palestine as are reflected in the Digests, these subordinates must have formed a constantly changing and socially unprotected group of men: men who could find no other work and must have been glad of even this thankless task; employees who were easily brought to engage in cheating from which they themselves would not profit.

The Digests (39, 4) make it clear that these customhouse employees were often not to be found at their booths when complaints were made of misconduct in the collection of the duties and taxes. The tax farmer had fired them or at least claimed to have done so. For this reason the Digests make the liability of the tax farmer explicitly clear: "Whether he has sold the slave or set him free or whether the slave has simply fled, the man who has kept such unsatisfactory servants is accountable for the slave's actions" (Dig. 39, 4, 13). The tax to be paid to the collectors was primarily the *portatorium,* which should not be thought of as a "tax" in the modern sense. It was a duty paid at the border but also in the interior:

> The *portatorium* corresponds to the old notion of a "toll" or "duty" and includes export duties levied on goods as they leave the duty-levying district, import duties levied on goods as they enter the district, transit duties paid for permission to take goods through a district, and even crossing-point duties (road and bridge tolls, fares, tolls at city gates) and market duties.[22]

Josephus, in *Antiquities* (17, 205; 18, 90), tells of market duties in Jerusalem that were introduced by Herod and strictly enforced and of others, again in Jerusalem, that were canceled by Vitellius in A.D. 36. The Tariff of Palmyra (a caravan city in the Syrian wilderness), a set of toll regulations passed by that city's council in A.D. 137, can in many respects be used also to shed light on conditions in Judea. The Tariff explains that duties are levied not only on luxury items imported from abroad but on every possible commodity: sheepskins, salted fish, wheat, wine, straw. "It was decreed that herbs should be subject to duty since they are articles of merchandise."[23] A duty must be paid on slaves that pass through the tollbooths. Even the prostitutes of the city must pay a toll: "The toll collector is also to require payment from a woman: a denarius from one who has taken a denarius or more, eight assarii from one who has taken eight assarii or more." Even the small craftsmen and shopkeepers in the city are not spared: a shoemaker must pay a denarius a month.[24] (At this time a denarius was, at best, worth only half as much as the denarius of Mt. 20:1ff.) The tax collectors were seemingly everywhere present, showing themselves wherever trade was being carried on or commodities were being transported; they were the scourge especially of tradesmen. The Palmyra Tariff speaks openly of the frequent quarrels between tradesmen and tax collectors.

The direct taxes levied by the Romans (taxes on crops; poll tax) were paid not to the tax collectors but to the Jewish authorities, who were supervised in this activity by the Roman procurator. Political conflicts with the Roman authorities seem to have arisen chiefly because of these direct taxes, less so because of duties.

MISCONDUCT BY TAX COLLECTORS

This seems to have been the order of the day. In the imperial period the state increasingly took steps to prevent such misconduct, but the steps could not have been completely effective. The tax collectors were under the control of officials of the state or the cities. From the time of Nero on, the list of duties in force at any time had to be posted in every toll both.[25] The Palmyra Tariff, too, was intended as a means of better controlling the tax collectors: "In former times many goods subject to duties were not explicitly listed in the tax regulations; instead duties were levied according to custom as written in the tax collector's contract"; therefore a detailed list of duties was now to be incised on a stone for public display. Despite these measures there were plenty of opportunities for deception and for collecting more than was due (Lk. 3:13; bSanh 25b), for example, by setting too high a value on the merchandise.

As a rule, a percentage of the value of the merchandise was to be paid as a tax. The *sykophantein* ("defraud") of which Zacchaeus accuses himself in Lk. 19:8, is a rather broad concept. In any case it has to do here with money collected unjustly at the toll booth. It might be, for example, that Zacchaeus as chief tax collector was in cahoots with the supervisory officials and would accuse customers at the toll booth of evading duties.[26]

Misconduct by tax collectors was punished; they were sentenced to pay a sum several times what they had gained. In Roman law a tax collector might be judged a thief and sentenced to make fourfold restitution (Dig. 39, 4), or he might have to make twofold restitution—the latter is viewed in Dig. 39, 4 as the usual punishment imposed on a tax collector for financial harm to a customer at the toll booth. On the other hand, it was possible for tax collectors, unlike thieves, to make voluntary restitution (Dig. 39, 4, 1. 4). In his changed state of mind, then, Zacchaeus was following the norms of Roman and (probably) ancient law generally in making fourfold restitution for theft.[27] It may be said, on the basis of Dig. 39, 4, that he was voluntarily declaring himself a thief, even though he did not have to. In fact, if the ancient reader of Lk. 19:8 was intended to see Zacchaeus as making some extraordinary gesture, the text would have had to make this explicitly clear. An ancient reader of this passage as it stands could have understood it to say only that the thieving tax collector was doing what he was legally bound to do; he was following legal prescription in making up for the harm he has done. The law did not, however, require that he give half of his possessions to the poor.

On the other hand, tradesmen and travelers were not entirely passive in face of the tax collectors. They could try to protect themselves against unjustified double duties by demanding receipts; bSab 78b presupposes such a case. The usual method, however, was to avoid duties by false declarations. For example, a man might claim that the slave accompanying him was in fact his son (bBB 127b). The harshest statement on tax evasion is in the Mishnah: "One may tell murderers, robbers, and tax collectors that something is due to a priest when it is not, or that it belongs to the king when it does not" (Ned 3, 4).

This passage of the Mishnah received divergent commentaries in the Babylonian Talmud: "Samuel said, however, that the law of the government is the law! R. Henana answered: This applies to a tax collector who has no limits set for him. The School of Rabbi Jannai explained it as referring to a tax collector who exploits" (bNed 28a; see bBK 113a). According to this passage, tax evasion is justified only when the tax collector does not have a tariff to follow or is not a tax collector at all but a rogue passing himself off as a tax collector. In our opinion, the Mishnah implies that at this period the abhorrence of duties and taxes also had nationalistic and political causes, since the justification it gives for tax evasion is either anarchic or an act of political resistance to foreign taxing agencies. In the first century, however, taxation does not seem to have been regarded so much as a political problem (see above).

CONTEMPT FOR TAX COLLECTORS

This was a widespread phenomenon in antiquity, but it calls for a nuanced appreciation. The nuances in question will emerge from some typical examples of texts on the inferior position of tax collector. But first a general thesis: moralists and jurists distinguished in their judgments between honorable and fraudulent tax collectors; educated people and people of rank scorned all tax collectors; and in any case tradesmen quarreled with tax collectors as to whether or not they were being cheated.

The passage already cited from the Babylonian Talmud can serve as one example of the distinctions made by moralists and jurists.[28] Another is the classification offered by Julius Pollux, a lexicographer of late antiquity. To someone who wants to curse a tax collector, Julius Pollux offers a wide selection of suitable insults indicating the tax collector's low moral status; these range from "monster" and "barefaced profiteer" to "robber." His list of laudatory terms for tax collectors is shorter but explicitly emphasizes their honesty: law-abiding, hospitable, fair, and so on (the praises are surely not ironic).[29]

It is obvious that tradesmen did not like tax collectors, even though the latter may not have particularly exploited them. Plutarch tells how disagreeable even a law-abiding tax collector seemed:

> People who interfere in the affairs of others and are curious are rightly hated. For example, we are outraged and incensed by tax collectors, not when they levy duties on objects displayed for them to see, but when they hunt out and rummage through what is hidden in people's baggage and in their loads of merchandise. And yet the law allows them to act in this way, and they would hurt themselves if they did not do it.[30]

Educated people and people of rank scorned all tax collectors and regarded them in principle as criminal, stupid, and unattractive. According to Philostratus, Apollonius the philosopher was crossing the border into Mesopotamia at Zeugma (bridge, river-crossing) when a toll collector asked him what he was bringing in with him. Apollonius answered: "I am bringing temperance, justice, virtue, continence, courage, discipline," and so on through a list of feminine abstract nouns. The toll collector smelled profit and said: "Please enter the names of your slave-women in the book." "Impossible," said Apollonius; "they are not slaves but ladies of rank."[31] The story reeks of the contempt that the educated felt for the uneducated; it resembles many of the jokes people tell today at the expense of the police.

To this third category also belong the many lists that have come down to us from antiquity, in which tax collectors are lumped together with criminals and other groups felt to be morally or esthetically offensive. These lists of despised trades are the most important evidence we have of the contempt in which tax collectors were held by socially respectable groups. Such lists cannot, of course, be taken without qualification as expressing popular feeling or, if you will, universal public opinion. We must always consider who is despising whom. Xenophon, for example, writes:

> For indeed those [arts] that are called mechanical [banausikoi—the very word already conveys contempt] are spoken against everywhere and have quite plausibly come by a very bad reputation in the cities. For they utterly ruin the bodies of those who work at them and those who are concerned with them, compelling them to sit still and remain indoors or in some cases even to spend the whole day by the fire. And when the bodies are made effeminate, the souls too become much more diseased. Lack of leisure to join in the concerns of friends and of the city is another condition of those that are called mechanical; those who practice them are reputed to be bad friends as well as bad defenders of their father-lands.[32]

The contempt shown here for manual workers comes from the owner of a large farming enterprise who sets a high value on his business for its productivity and contribution to the state and considers the fresh air he breathes to be a just reward for his aristocratic status.

This example of the contempt in which manual workers were held should make it evident how unjust the lists of despised trades were. In the case of tax collectors and prostitutes we are rather inclined to accept the judgment of ancient society; in the case of manual workers, however, we find it extremely difficult. The question of who is despising whom is important in relation to the Jesus tradition and its stories about Jesus as friend of tax collectors, because it helps to draw the lines more clearly. What is it that Jesus the friend of tax collectors is rejecting: a general and justified antipathy toward tax collectors or, much more specifically, the arrogance of the refined folk who reproach the fugitive slave for being dirty and a criminal?

The list of despised trades, which include tax collectors, exemplifies that kind of social arrogance: "Swineherds, small tradesmen, leasers of fruit crops, fruit sellers, tax gatherers—who collect tithes and twentieths and fiftieths—, customs agents at ports, town criers, sailors, innkeepers, ferrymen, procurers, servants, tanners, garlic sellers."[33] All these were poorly paid jobs in the service sector and were filled by the poor. Well-to-do individuals made use of these people and despised them.

Documents that speak specifically of the place of tax collectors in Jewish society give a rather nuanced picture.[34] The Mishnah outlaws not tax collectors but (only) the money in their cashboxes. Such money is not to be used in moneychanging, nor may one accept it as alms (BK 10, 1, 2). Like the passage (Ned 3, 4) already cited from the Mishnah, this one probably reflects the fact that the scribes in the age of the Mishnah, unlike those of the first century, were rejecting the political implications of taxes. We hear of a tax collector who was scorned by the councillors of his city, but we also hear of a prosperous tax collector who was numbered among the dignitaries of his city.[35] We are told of pious men who did not think a tax collector capable of good works,[36] but there is no basis for assuming a general depreciation of tax collectors by the Pharisees, much less by the Jewish populace as a whole.

The harshest depreciation of tax collectors is to be found in the Babylonian Talmud, bSanh 25b. The passage goes beyond the Mishnah and states that herdsmen and collectors of taxes and duties are unacceptable as witnesses and judges. This decision represented a radical deprivation of rights. The compilers fully realized, however, that this measure was adopted only at a time later than the Mishnah and that it required a juridical justification: "It was originally thought that collectors of taxes and duties took only what was determined by law; when it was seen, however, that they took more, they were declared unacceptable." In a now classic essay on the question of tax collectors and sinners in the Gospels, Joachim Jeremias surely draws overly broad conclusions from bSanh 25b when he generalizes from the popular ostracism of tax collectors and speaks without qualification of their ostracism by law.[37]

On the whole, then, the thesis enunciated earlier may be taken as valid even for Jewish society: jurists and moralists condemned tax collectors *only* when they did wrong; tradesmen always attacked them; educated people and people of rank despised them as a body.

When Luke (18:9-14) tells of the Pharisee being contemptuous of the tax collector and lumping him together with extortioners, the unjust, and adulterers, he is not describing the real situation in first-century Palestine. Rather, he is using the Pharisee to depict the arrogant attitude that respectable Christians in his community adopted toward tax collectors and other despised criminal or even noncriminal but poorly paying trades.

The poor (the *ptochoi*) and even day laborers and fugitive slaves did not have to pay duties, because they had nothing on which duties could be levied. The quarrels between tradesmen and tax collectors must have been a matter of indifference to them; they had other cares. In fact, they would hardly have been among those who despised tax collectors.

2. Sinners

If we are to understand what the word "sinners" (*Hamartoloi*) means in the earliest Jesus tradition, we must put aside the latter theological definitions of this concept, such as we already find in Luke. As almost everyone acknowledges, "sinners" designates a particular group of people that is to be defined in sociological terms. Such a view of the word is already imposed by the linkage of "tax collectors" and "sinners." Two definitions in particular of the term "sinner" have been debated: it refers to the *'am hā'āres,* or to the practitioners of despised trades.

In the first and second centuries A.D. Pharisaic Jews scornfully dismissed non-pharisaic Jews as *'am hā'āres*. In the first century the Pharisees were as yet a small group, and in their eyes, therefore, the majority of the people were *'am hā'āres*. At this period the concept of *'am hā'āres,* does not seem to have had any special sociological content. Those leading a non-pharisaic life included not only uneducated people whose poverty made study of the Torah impossible, but also rich Jews who may have studied the Torah but not in the Pharisaic manner and were therefore regarded by the Pharisees as "uneducated" or *'am hā'āres*. Only when the Pharisees took over the leadership of the Jewish people in the second century did this polemical Pharisaic notion become a weapon in the hands of the powerful. Those few Jews who did not accept Pharisaic claims to leadership were boycotted by society and soon became social outcasts.[38]

Jeremias in particular has shown convincingly that the "sinners " of the Jesus tradition did not belong to the *'am hā'āres*: "It must be noticed, above all, that Jesus himself was *'am hā'āres* in the eyes of the Pharisees . . . . But there was nothing scandalous about a member of *'am hā'āres* associating with his fellows."[39] We can therefore no longer identify "sinners" and *'am hā'āres*, nor can we assume that the Pharisees were in a special degree despisers of "sinners."

Jeremias has therefore assumed that "sinners," like tax collectors, were practitioners of despised trades and that the contempt felt for them was shared by the people at large. In addition (he says), in the case of sinners we must think of people "whose immoral way of life was common knowledge, such as adulterers, prostitutes, murderers, robbers, and swindlers."[40] But in fact it is hardly to be assumed that "sinners," like tax collectors, practiced despised trades. First of all, the lists of such trades cannot generally be regarded as reflecting popular opinion; in addition, the lists must be approached in a nuanced way, as we saw above. Second, and above all, the followers of Jesus must have regarded that kind of ostracism as unjust. They would surely not have accepted such a judgment on "sinners"; and yet it seems that even in the earliest Jesus tradition the Jesus people themselves used the concept "sinner," since nowhere is there any trace of a coolness toward this judgment of the adversaries of Jesus.

The most likely hypothesis is that "sinners" were criminals and guilty even in the eyes of Jesus' disciples. By "criminals" we may understand concretely those who not only practiced despised trades but also had in fact committed one or other of the crimes to which people thought them liable by reason of their trades. Criminals included, for example, herdsmen who pastured their sheep in fields belonging to others. It is doubtful, on the other hand, that prostitutes and adulterers were described as "sinners" in the earliest Jesus movement, since in that tradition "sinners" stand alongside tax collectors and prostitutes (Mt. 11:19, Q; 21:31; Mk. 2:13–17); "sinners" is not a generic term that includes tax collectors and prostitutes.

It is not until Luke that we find such an expanded concept of sinner. Thus he calls a prostitute "a woman of the city, who was a sinner" (Lk. 7:37) and in general uses the term "sinner" in a very inclusive sense. For him tax collectors exemplify those whom superior folk despise on moral and social grounds, while concrete "sinners" exemplify the situation of human beings before God. It is for this theological reason that he uses the word "sinners"; he does not on that account make the position of the despisers his own. But the word "sinner" cannot have had this meaning in the earliest Jesus tradition, because Jesus himself was not yet understood in soteriological terms; he was not yet the redeemer of human beings, who are all sinful in God's eyes.

3. Prostitutes

We return to surer ground when we inquire into the meaning of the word *porné* ("prostitute"). Matthew 21:31 has the combination "tax collectors and prostitutes"; the saying probably comes from the earliest Jesus tradition. Luke does not say with equal explicitness that Jesus took the part of tax collectors and prostitutes, but he knows of this tradition, since he tells the stories of the woman who was a great sinner (Lk. 7:36–50) and of the tax collectors (Lk. 18:9ff.; 19:1ff.). That the sinful woman was a prostitute (and not an adulteress) is to be assumed on the basis of 7:47 ("she loved much"), although the ancient mind hardly distinguished between adulteresses and prostitutes. In many regions, in fact, adulteresses were forced into prostitution as a punishment.[41]

The sinful woman in Luke used an expensive perfumed oil. At the Palmyra city limits a relatively heavy duty had to be paid on flasks of such oil: 25 denarii on a camel-load of them.[42] Luke is probably thinking of a well-groomed, "high-class" prostitute who could afford the most expensive perfumed oil.

The vast majority of prostitutes, however, especially in the cities of the Roman empire, including the cities of Palestine,[43] were a wretched lot. In general, their services were sold by procurers in brothels. The procurers were often not the owners of the brothels, but slaves or freedmen of the owners; the latter preferred to appear before the public as men of honor.[44] The prostitutes were usually slaves whom the procurer bought for his brothel. If they had not been slaves from birth, it was economic necessity that turned them into prostitutes: parents sold or rented their daughters for this purpose.[45] Female infants exposed at birth and women captured in war formed a reservoir of talent for the profiteers in prostitution.[46]

4. Beggars, the Poor, and Cripples

The word used for "poor" in the Gospels is the Greek word *ptōchos,* not *penēs*. In Greek a *ptōchos* is someone who is destitute, where as a *penēs* is a poor person who must earn his living by his own unremitting toil. To the educated upper class of Athens anyone who had to work and had no leisure to cultivate physical fitness was "poor."[47] In the heyday of Athens beggars were a rare exception, but in the Roman empire of the first century A.D. destitution was the condition of a sizable part of the population, both rural and urban. Doubtless, then, the word used for "poor" in the Gospel accurately reflects the social situation.

It is clear in all strata of the Jesus tradition that when the synoptic Gospels speak of the "poor" (= *ptōchoi*) they are in fact thinking of extreme want and often even of destitution. The "poor" are named as recipients of alms (Mk. 10:21 par.); Lazarus the poor man is a sick beggar (pre-Lucan Lk. 16:19ff.); and the beggars who are fetched for the great banquet are both the local poor and sick and the itinerant beggars who hang about outside the villages (Lk. 14:21, 23).[48]

But though the "poor" are mentioned in the same breath with the sick in the earliest Jesus tradition (Mt. 11:2–5 par.Q/older than Q) and though poverty is synonymous with hunger and lamentation (Lk. 6:20f.; see also Lk. 1:46ff.), these "poor" are not necessarily beggars in the strict sense, that is, persons who economically are completely dependent on help from others. The reference can also be to starving groups a cut "above" beggary: unemployed day laborers, fugitive slaves, or individuals rendered homeless by economic forces, as, for example, small farmers driven into an economic corner by burdensome taxes, crop failures, or debt. This kind of poverty was widespread throughout the Roman empire; even in imperial Rome itself, despite a well-organized public system of grain distribution, there were many destitute people.[49]

In first-century Palestine the economic condition of the population as a whole seems to have been bad. An important indicator of this is the civil wars that repeatedly flared up and the attempted revolts against Rome. Economic, political, and religious distress went together. Insurgents could always find plenty of what Josephus calls *aporoi,* people in a hopeless economic situation, who would take part in an uprising. In this context Josephus' account in the *Jewish War* (2, 425ff.) has drawn a great deal of attention. At the beginning of the war in A.D. 66 the rebels burned the records office in Jerusalem and destroyed the debenture bonds of creditors in order to "make impossible the recovery of debts [and] secure the support of an army of debtors and enable the poor (*aporoi*) to rise with impunity against the rich (*euporoi*)."[50]

When Vespasian captured Tarichea (in Galilee, A.D. 67), he spared the native residents, but the masses of homeless people (Josephus gives figures of up to 40,000), fugitives, rebels, and criminals were killed, imprisoned, or sold, because Vespasian regarded them as a force for political unrest.[51] Josephus describes in gruesome detail the mass deaths of the starving in beleaguered Jerusalem: vast numbers of corpses of the poor were dragged outside the city or, when this was no longer possible, were heaped up in large houses.[52]

But there are also reports about the first decades of the first century that imply the impoverishment of large sectors of the population. Herod Antipas (4 B.C.–A.D. 39), for example, built the city of Tiberias for himself and forced people to inhabit it; the latter consisted in part of beggars gathered from the entire country. The reign of Herod the Great is described as marked by a sharp contrast between magnificent buildings and fortresses, on the one hand, and the economic decline of the population, on the other. "Depriving them of their old prosperity and their ancestral laws he had reduced his people to poverty and utter lawlessness." The great famines under Herod in 25 B.C. and in Jerusalem in A.D. 46–48 seem to have been due to structural causes rather than to chance. [53] There are reports of a lack of seed for sowing, a lack of grain, people dead of starvation, and plagues. The drought before the start of the famine under Herod triggered the catastrophe but was hardly its root cause. We can imagine the long-term effects of such famines (e.g., the ruin of small farmers).

When the Jesus tradition speaks of the "poor," it is not possible in individual cases to say whether the reference is to beggars, impoverished rural folk, unemployed day laborers, or other groups of people who have turned itinerant for some other motive and are in "flight for social reasons."[54] But to the extent that the tradition originated in Palestine, the reference is doubtless to the poverty to which Josephus likewise calls attention in various contexts. If we assemble the most important data in the synoptic Gospels, it becomes clear that they convey reliable information about the human social situation. Consider, for example, the interchangeableness of the terms "poverty" and "hunger" (in Athens, on the contrary, it was "poverty" and "work" that went together); the illustration of poverty by scenes of begging; the linking of poverty and sickness.

Luke's description of the scene in Acts 3:1-11 is doubtless not a historical account, but it very likely provides an accurate picture of historical reality. The crippled beggar sits in front of the temple of Jerusalem; the disciples of Jesus cannot give him money because they have none. They do, however, cure him—and this too may reflect historical fact (even if the cure is not supernatural in a dogmatically inflected sense). It is unimportant whether Luke received the story from tradition or gave an intuitively accurate presentation of it. Though he did not know Palestine he could imagine the scene because the condition of the poor was not much better in his own country than it had been in Palestine in the time of Jesus.

III. JESUS, HOPE OF THE POOR

1. Reflections on Method

Before an interpretation of the earliest Jesus tradition can be given on the basis of the sociohistorical information thus far presented, the method for investigating and establishing this level of the tradition must be sketched. We must bear in mind that this earliest tradition has already been incorporated into continuous literary entities (Q; Mark; Matthew; Luke) and assimilated to these new contexts. The first step in getting behind these documents, which from a literary viewpoint are clearly self-contained, is taken by redaction criticism. That is, we have to be able to distinguish the conception of the evangelists or Q from the content of a saying, a text, or a connected series of texts. Only then will it be possible to speak persuasively of a pre-Lucan, pre-Matthean, and pre-Marcan tradition that has been secondarily incorporated into the Gospels. The same path of redaction criticism can then be traveled anew in investigating and establishing the earliest tradition about Jesus as reflected in the Sayings-source.

In this way we reach the relatively earliest stage of tradition that lies behind individual texts or groups of texts that are related from a literary standpoint; this does not make it possible, of course, to locate this relatively earliest tradition in a historical sequence. For example, pre-Marcan tradition need not yet be the absolutely earliest tradition about Jesus. The search for the earliest tradition in this sense must therefore be supplemented by a search for a "life context" (Sitz im Leben) for the texts in question. We need to ask whether the history of religions, the history of ideas, and social history can provide clues that permit us to relate the text to the earliest Jesus movement in Palestine. ("Life context" must therefore be taken in the widest possible sense: the context provided by the life of the society as such; the Sitz im Leben is a "sociological context"). Once we have gained at least a partial insight into the earliest Jesus movement, we can relate to this stratum of tradition other texts that display the same presuppositions and fit materially into the picture already developed.

It is quite possible, of course, to suggest considerations that challenge this conclusion. For example, why should not materially related traditions have arisen both in the earliest Jesus movement and in a Jewish-Christian group (circa A.D. 70)? Critical reflections of this kind are abundantly possible. More evidence than what has been described above is not to be had. Proofs that can stand up to any attack are not to be found. Criteria for determining the earliest Jesus tradition—or, if one regards the question as possible, for the words of the historical Jesus—will always (and not just in the course followed in this book) be the result of preliminary decisions regarding method. In this book the history of traditions provides one approach; an investigation of the life context of these traditions by way of a form-critical study that has been expanded to include social history provides the other.[55]

Despite its hypothetical character, the reconstruction of the earliest Jesus tradition yields a doubtless fragmentary but nonetheless suggestive picture of the earliest Jesus movement. Concretely, the most important steps are the following. It can be shown that Lk. 6:20f. is already used secondarily in the Sayings-source. Matthew 11:2-5,Q is likewise older than the Sayings-source.[56] Both texts understand the presence of Jesus as the coming of salvation to the poor; both reflect expectation of the reign of God. They have other points in common as well. They already allow us to infer the existence of a Jesus movement within Judaism long before the destruction of Jerusalem in A.D. 70. They give a glimpse into a unique world of ideas that is pregnant with the future.

These important texts can be correlated with others that are similar in content and satisfy the same traditio-historical requirements. In what follows, the purpose is not to give as complete a picture as possible of the earliest Jesus tradition but, rather, to grasp the meaning of the major texts of the earliest Jesus tradition.[57] Here two themes are central: the wretched lot of the poor will be reversed under the reign of God, and Jesus is friend of tax collectors and sinners. We shall turn first to the texts dealing with the hope of the poor.

2. The Beatitude of the Poor

The most important text of the earliest Jesus tradition is the Beatitude regarding the poor. We may assume that the Lucan version in Lk. 6:20f. has largely preserved the form the text had in the earliest Jesus tradition; we come therefore to the following reconstruction:

> Blessed the poor,
>> for the kingdom of God is theirs.
> Blessed the hungry,
>> for they shall be filled.
> Blessed those who weep
>> for [they shall laugh].

Grounds for the reconstruction are as follows: it is impossible to reach ultimate certainty on whether the direct-address form of Luke ("yours is the kingdom of God") or the statement form of Matthew ("theirs is the kingdom of God") is to be assumed for the earliest tradition. The material meaning of the text is not affected by the decision on this point; even in the statement form the poor can still be the addressees. An argument for the statement form is provided by Mk. 10:14: "Let the children come to me, do not hinder them; for to such belongs the kingdom of God"—which is likewise a saying of Jesus that can be claimed for the earliest Jesus tradition.

The Sayings-source had already added the Beatitude of the persecuted disciples (Lk. 6:22f., Q) to the Beatitudes in Lk. 6:20ff. The result was to give beatitudes as a whole a different meaning: it was now not the poor but the poor persecuted disciples of Jesus who were being declared blessed. The peculiarities of the Beatitudes in Matthew (5:3-12), especially the addition of *tō pneumati* ("the poor in spirit"), indicate later revisions that are due in part to Matthew himself. We need not consider these points here.

The Beatitudes as found in the earliest Jesus tradition presuppose that Jesus is the Messiah of the last times, whose presence fulfills the biblical prophecies and marks the dawning of the reign of God. Isaiah 61:1—"He has sent me to bring good news to the poor"—is now understood as a prophecy that is fulfilled in the preachng of Jesus. When Jesus says, "Blessed (*makarioi*) are the poor" the promised good news (*euangelizesthai*) becomes a reality. In Mt. 11:5 Jesus answers the Baptist's question, "Are you he who is to come, or shall we look for another?" by saying, ". . . tell John what you hear and see: the blind receive their sight and the lame walk, lepers are cleansed and the deaf hear, and the dead are raised up, and the poor have good news preached to them." This text too belongs to the earliest Jesus tradition and says materially the same thing as the Beatitude of the poor. The presence of Jesus already brings the beginning of God's reign. The poor hear the message of God's reign and their situation is already altered thereby, no less than that of the blind whom Jesus miraculously heals. The Beatitudes of the poor presuppose faith in Jesus: his coming is the beginning of God's reign. It is theoretically possible that the historical-human-being Jesus understood himself as Messiah in this sense, but a judgment on this point is beyond the capabilities of historical reconstruction.

The reign of God is expected in the future (the hungry *shall* be filled), but it is also something present, since experience of it is already possible. Let us try to imagine for ourselves the situation of the disciples of Jesus as we hear of it in this earliest tradition. In Palestine, perhaps already in the lifetime of Jesus, perhaps afterward as well, poor Jews are congregating as followers of Jesus. They see their own condition of poverty[58]—marked by hunger and tears and probably sickness—as a scandal in God's sight. That kind of wretched life is not from God, who will soon put an end to such disorder. God will assert divine rule, and then hunger and the suffering of poverty will be things of the past. The disciples of Jesus are certainly poor themselves, and they bring the good news to other poor people. The presence of this promise is already causing many changes. Miracles are occurring. We cannot doubt that in the Jesus movement human beings were healed and that they understood these marvels as marking the beginning of the last times.

In Lk. 6:20f. the reign or kingdom of God is awaited; we must, however, examine more closely what this means. How do these disciples of Jesus represent the salvation for which they hope? Satisfaction (being filled) and laughter: divergent notions come together here in the picture of salvation. In the environment from which these texts spring, satisfaction and laughter are the typical condition of the rich (see, e.g., Lk. 16:19; 6:25). The elements of satisfaction and laughter are also to be found in religious representations of salvation in antiquity: experiences of encounter with God are described in terms of joy,[59] while salvation is thought of as a banquet in the kingdom of God (see, e.g., Lk. 22:30).

But it is the present experience of poverty, hunger, and tears that plays the decisive part in determining the object of hope. The hope is not simply that this condition of distress will come to an end; it is for much more: complete compensation, a complete indemnification for former privation. Present wretchedness is not thought of as provisional, superficial, or unimportant in light of the end and by comparison with the end-state; rather, it is taken seriously in determining the very content or object of hope. The wretchedness is not a passing thing that will be as though it had never been; rather, the coming happiness will be as glorious as the present distress is grim and gloomy. The ability to think in utopian terms is a creative power. Our theological tradition has made us too quick to remove all the color from this picture of hope. These people had very concrete things in mind when they thought of the kingdom of God as a future in which they would be satisfied and able to laugh. Perhaps they already saw the marvelous foods on the table: the choice bread baked with flour and oil, the eggs, honey, and wine—all the things that made for a festive meal.

3. The Disconcerting Quality and the Meaning of the Earliest Jesus Tradition

We must not cover up the aspects of the Jesus movement that we find disconcerting; otherwise we shall not really come to grips with what the figure of Jesus meant and still means. We find it disconcerting, first of all, that human beings should expect the reign of God to bring a complete transformation of the world and history. We also find disconcerting the expectation of the poor that their lot will be reversed: that their tears will turn into laughter, their hunger into satisfaction. Such a hope not only makes us conscious of confronting an alien worldview (we do not expect the kind of reign of God that these people did). It also spurs criticism of its content: Does not such a hope stultify the poor and fill them with a false consolation, even as it renders them passive? Or else we give our critique of the content a theological formulation: Does not such a hope turn God into a tool of people filled with resentment, into a fulfiller of unfulfilled wishes? It is psychologically understandable, of course, that the hungry should cultivate such notions; more than this we cannot say in defense of such a hope.

In addition, we find the miracles disconcerting. We can indeed imagine hope making poor sick human beings strong and active once again. But we do not regard this as a miracle in the supernatural sense as they did.

The meaning of the following of Jesus cannot be that we must make these disconcerting notions our own to the fullest possible extent and that we must give the name "faith" to the strain such an effort imposes. That would be to turn the life-giving activities of a former age into a dogma that we today find estranged from life. Let us therefore be permitted for once to use this central text of the earliest Jesus tradition as the occasion and basis for rendering explicit, even if very briefly, the directions implicit in the text. After all, while this book is an attempt to understand the historical past and not a book on faith in our day, the two cannot be neatly and tidily separated from one another.

We can attempt to bring alive for ourselves the hopes and practice of that earliest following of Jesus: to express these in our language and our images and in actions that fit our situation. We can and even must do this, because this way (whether or not it be thought of as a following of Jesus) is the only way out of the helpless cynicism that leaves in the hands of brutal power all decisions about human life today and in the future. Concretely, we hope that there will be a future in which the powerful will no longer prevail over the weak; that it will forevermore be wrong to endanger and kill human beings and to cheat them of life. We call this hope a hope in the reign of God, a hope that human beings need not be hopeless in the face of their own weakness. We believe that the poor and the weak can work miracles for one another.

Some, inspired by certain theological presuppositions, will object to this "transposition" of the following of Jesus that it says "too little," too little in the sense that the following of Jesus is here limited to the this-worldly, social, and even political sphere. The objection may be valid. But the "more" that can be added to what has been said must not be allowed to suppress the "little." For by any accounting the Gospels that describe the following of Jesus show a determined interest in the activities of these followers. They do not contrast Christological statements about Jesus with the concrete behavior of his followers so as to turn this behavior into something insignificant. A future judgment based on the actions of human beings is a central idea in the New Testament; it has become a forgotten theme in our theological tradition.

Finally, we also find disconcerting the woe-sayings against the rich (Lk. 6:24–26). It is no longer possible to say with certainty whether these were already a part of the earliest Jesus tradition. In any event, the theological problem they raise arises even for the earliest Jesus tradition. How did that tradition deal with the rich? Did the first followers dream of revenge or desire the punishment of the rich? This question is already implicit in Lk. 6:20f. The poor, it is said there, will inherit the kingdom of God. Will they alone inherit it? We can tell, as we listen to the Beatitude of the poor, that even if the woe-sayings against the rich were added only later on, they nonetheless draw appropriate conclusions from the Beatitude itself. We must return to this question further on when we are in a position to survey all the material on the eschatological reversal of the lots of poor and rich.

4. The Camel-saying

The Beatitude of the poor is not an isolated aphorism in the earliest Jesus tradition, although it does indeed convey the central message of the disciples of Jesus. The Gospels also contain material parallels, which are so close in content to the Beatitudes that we may consider them part of the earliest tradition, especially since the traditio-historical requirements for such a classification are present in all cases. These parallels are the camel-saying in Mk. 10:25; the saying about the first and the last, which has been transmitted in several contexts; the Magnificat in Lk. 1:46–55; and (probably) the story of the rich man and Lazarus the poor man (Lk. 16:19–26).

"It is easier for a camel to go through the eye of a needle than for a rich man to enter the kingdom of God" (Mk. 10:25). Mark transmits this stern saying in the course of a conversation that Jesus and his disciples have on the problem of the rich, after the "rich young man" has refused to follow Jesus. We must give Mark credit for transmitting this saying even though he himself and his community could not identify with it and must have found it alarming. This is clear in particular from Mk. 10:26 where the shock of the disciples is expressly mentioned. The Marcan community lived in a social situation completely different from that reflected in the earliest Jesus tradition. Rich Christians too now belonged to the community. It is not possible in our present context to examine Mk. 10:17-31 and the Marcan judgment on the renunciation of property,[60] since we are concerned here only with Mk. 10:25.

In its present textual form the verse is even pre-Marcan. It has occasionally been suggested that in its original form the saying did not speak of a "rich man" but said simply that the human being as such can enter the kingdom of God only with infinite difficulty or even cannot enter it at all by his or her own powers.[61] In this view, Mark subsequently transformed the original saying of Jesus into a hard saying about the rich. This hypothesis breaks down due to the fact that Mark of all people has no interest in rendering still more tense the Christian attitude to the rich. The whole context of Jesus' conversation with the disciples (Mk. 10:23-31), coming as it does after the story of the rich young man, shows in its every sentence that Mark's own position is different from that expressed in Mk. 10:25.

These attempts to reconstruct an original text for Mk. 10:25 that does not pass judgment on the rich reflect once again the difficulties that Christians today, as in the time of Mark, find with this saying. Surely (they think) it cannot be said in the name of Jesus that the rich are excluded from the kingdom of God. (The paradoxical picture of the huge camel and the tiny needle's eye means, after all, that the entrance of the rich is impossible—not that it is simply difficult, as Mark tries to make it mean in 10:23.) Even the position reflected in the story of the rich young man—which is also probably pre-Marcan—is not that radical. It tells indeed of a failed invitation to renunciation of property, but on the whole it is intended to encourage the rich to become followers and renounce their property. Mark 10:25, however, represents a different outlook. It is not concerned with renunciation of property. It does not even voice a threat but is simply an eschatological prophecy like the "woe" against the rich in Lk. 6:24. It demands nothing of the rich: not repentance, not renunciation of property. It predicts the future of the rich. It complements the Beatitude of the poor and is probably part of the earliest Jesus tradition. The basis for the prediction can probably be found in Lk. 6:24, where it is said that the rich remain outside because in their lifetime they have already had what will be given in the kingdom.

The camel-saying is striking for the unemotional way in which it refrains from any prediction of punishment or revenge. A comparison will bring out this quality. In Ethiopic Enoch those now oppressed announce God's judgment on those now in power: "Do know that you shall be given over into the hands of the righteous ones, and they shall cut off your necks and slay you, and they shall not have compassion on you" (98, 182).[62] The comparison is invoked here only to bring out the unique character of Mk. 10:25, and not to show early Christianity as the superior religion next to which other religions are seen only as a dark "background." The threat that Ethiopic Enoch levels against the rich must likewise be understood in the context of its concrete situation, but that is something we are not concerned with here.

5. The Last Will Be First

"The last will be first, and the first last." This saying, cited here in the version given in Mt. 20:16, is transmitted on four occasions: Mk. 10:31; Mt. 19:30; Mt. 20:16; Lk. 13:30.

The context in which the saying appears in the Gospels is established in each instance by the evangelists themselves: first, by Mark in 10:31[63] and therefore also by Matthew in 19:30. Matthew then uses it again in 20:16, while the use made of it in Lk. 13:30 is Lucan. Luke uses the saying to threaten Christian malefactors who are self-righteous and avaricious. In any event the saying is older than its present contexts, and its original meaning is not to be derived from these contexts.

The wording of the ancient saying is most likely to have been the one cited from Mt. 20:16. The restrictive versions ("Many that are first . . . " in Mk. 10:31 and Mt. 19:30; Lk. 13:30 also has a restrictive version: "Behold, some are last who . . . ") are to be explained as the result of subsequent reflection on an originally sweeping saying.

The meaning of the old saying seems at first glance difficult to determine; it seems susceptible of several interpretations. Some have therefore assumed that it is a variant of an ancient proverb and means "How easily fortune changes overnight."[64] But as far as we know, the saying is not documented as a proverb; moreover, the future tense would be odd in a proverb with this meaning. The unusual character of the future here emerges with special clarity when we compare parallel motifs—numerous in antiquity—dealing with the reversal of human destinies. The parallel motifs that seem to provide the best analogies will be discussed here, because the comparison makes it all the clearer that the saying was perhaps an early Christian "saying on wandering" but not an ancient proverb or a cliché. It became a cliché only in the Christian *post*history of the Gospels.

In ancient documents we find it frequently said that the divinity has power to exalt the lowly and humble the mighty. This reference to the power of the divinity often serves as a warning to the powerful not to misuse their power.[65] The motif of the reversal of social fortunes is also common in texts that express fear of a coming chaos, a revolution. An upheaval of the social order, with top and bottom exchanging places, is an object of anxiety regarding the future: "And many will be delivered to the few, those who were nothing will rule over the strong, the poor will be greater in number than the rich, and the impious will exalt themselves over the brave" (Syriac Baruch 70:4).[66] But these fears of revolution and chaos, fears which at times are even apocalyptic in character, are simply parallels that in fact shed no light in our present context.

Serious parallels are to be found only in the few texts that make a social reversal the object of *hope,* for in the context of early Christianity the saying about the first and last was certainly an expression of hope, not of fear or threat; only Luke uses it as a threat or warning. Xenophon, for example, in *Anabasis* III, 2, 10, encourages the numerically inferior Greeks to defend themselves against Persian military superiority by telling them that the gods can quickly make even the strong weak and, if it be their will, can rescue the weak. In Aristophanes' *Lysistrata* an oracle, which promises that distress will end and far-thundering Zeus will lay the mighty low, is intended to encourage the women to unite and win a victory over their husbands who are bitten by the bug of war. Aristophanes himself, of course, makes vulgar fun of this feminine hope, (*Lysistrata* 772f.).

To us today with our modern cultural background it may seem obvious that the saying about the first and the last is a proverb or an equivocal saying about wandering, but, as the brief exposition of parallel motifs shows, this interpretation is completely erroneous. In the context of early Christianity the saying is an eschatological prophecy that has the earliest Jesus tradition for its proximate setting and in its own way makes the statement we already saw made in Lk. 6:20f. As for the parallel passages in Xenophon and Aristophanes, it must be noted that they seek to induce a desired form of behavior (courage in war; unity among women) by appealing to hope in the support of the gods. It turns out, then, that despite numerous parallel motifs, texts whose content is analogous to the saying in Mt. 20:16 or, more generally, to the idea of an eschatological reversal of social destinies have not been found in ancient literature.

The last will be first. "First" and "last" refer to social locations, to "above" and "below" in the social sense.[67]

Those who are last now will be first in the kingdom of God, and those who are powerful now and first in society will have lowly places in the kingdom of God. Here again we must try to imagine the concrete notions that accompanied this generalization; for example, the notion that the poor who eke out a miserable existence amid illness and hunger on the roads of Palestine will then be healthy and clean and will have the places of honor at table.

6. The Rich Man and the Poor Lazarus

The story of the rich man and the poor Lazarus is likewise to be assigned to the earliest Jesus tradition. Here are the most important arguments for saying so:

a) Luke 16:19–26 is pre-Lucan, since Lk. 16:27-31 is a later Lucan reinterpretation of the material; this reinterpretation takes the form of a continuation of the story, but the focus has now changed, being on the conversion of the rich. This new theme is not present, even implicitly, in Lk. 19:19–26, because the aim of the story is to depict not some wrong behavior on the part of the rich man (e.g., that he has failed to give alms to Lazarus), but the consequences of his comfortable life, as 16:25 explicitly says: "Son, remember that you in your lifetime received your good things, and Lazarus in like manner evil things; but now he is comforted here, and you are in anguish." We must follow the flow of the story: it leads to 16:25. If the story had for its aim to depict some misconduct of the rich man, it would say so. Instead it depicts his comfortable life and its terrible and unalterable consequences. The "abyss" in the other world shows how unalterable this future destiny is.

b) There are numerous parallel motifs, especially in an Egyptian-Hellenistic story, but we know of no parallel that is analogous in content to Lk. 16:19–26.

In interpreting Lk. 16:19–31, H. Gressmann[68] appeals to the Egyptian-Hellenistic story of the journey of Setme Chamois and his son Si-osiris through the world of the dead; this story tells of a social reversal in the next life.[69]

According to the story, a poor man who has died is simply wrapped in a mat and carried unceremoniously into the desert. A rich man, on the other hand, is carried amid loud lamentations and signs of great respect to the desert necropolis; there he is entombed along with many costly objects for his use in the next world. The father and son are spectators at both funerals. The father remarks how much better off the rich are than the poor. But the son, who possesses wonderful insight, says to this father: "May you enjoy the same lot in the kingdom of the dead that this poor man enjoys." To prove his point he leads his father through the kingdom of the dead. There they see that the poor man has been given the burial clothing and gifts of the rich man; he is clad in a linen robe and enjoys a privileged position "near the place where Osiris was." The rich man, on the other hand, is in torment: the hinge of the gate to the realm of the dead has penetrated his right eye, and his mouth is continually open in a loud cry of pain. The deeds of both men have been weighed in the kingdom of the dead: the good deeds of the poor man were more numerous than his evil deeds, and the evil deeds of the rich man were more numerous than his good deeds. Therefore their lots in the world of the dead are reversed. The story does not say what the evil deeds of the rich man or the good deeds of the poor man were. The moral of the story is that at the judgment of the dead the deeds of human beings are weighed without respect for persons.

"No distinction is made there between rich and poor; they alone are honored who are found to be without fault." The intention of the story, according to Gressmann, is to criticize the idea that one's condition in the realm of the dead is, in principle, a continuation of one's condition in the present life.[70] This is the outlook represented in the story by the father when he is outraged by his son's statement at the burial of the rich man and the poor man ("May you enjoy the same lot in the kingdom of the dead that this poor man enjoys"); he can only conceive of this wish as malicious. The purpose of the story, then, is to show that the judgment of the dead is based on the deeds done in this life.

In its content, then, this story exemplifies the use of the motif of social reversal as an argument in ethical exhortations, except that, unlike the texts discussed earlier, the story has retribution for evil deeds being inflicted exclusively after death. This story and Lk. 16:19–26 are comparable only to the extent that they employ related narrative motifs. Content, intention, and function differ radically in the two stories. The Egyptian story says: There is a judgment that is based on deeds and pays no heed to the individual's social position. Luke 16 says: There will be compensation for the wretchedness of the poor.

Here again we see that the idea of an eschatological reversal of social destinies is unparalleled in the history of ideas and religions.

c) The problems raised by the content of Lk. 16:19–26 in the context of the earliest Jesus tradition must be faced, but they can be resolved. One problem is that the reign of God seems to play no role here and that attention is focused instead on the future lot that *the individual* will enjoy after death in the bosom of Abraham or in hell, as the case may be. These two conceptions (Abraham's bosom/hell and the kingdom of God) have nothing to do with one another; they cannot be equated. The second problem is that we cannot overlook the fact that in Lk. 16:19–26 the rich man is punished. This idea that the rich will be punished cannot be found, at least with the same harshness, elsewhere in the earliest tradition. (For more on this point, see below.)

The disparity between the two eschatologies can, however, be explained. In the context of the earliest Jesus movement the story would have to be understood as a parable. Luke himself, for that matter, understands it as a parable, even though he does not formally present it as such. The parable has for its purpose to explain the eschatological reversal of social destinies in the kingdom of God by showing the fate of a single rich man and a single poor man after death.

The arguments just summarized, showing that Lk. 16:19–26 belongs to the earliest tradition, are weighty ones. One problem remains: the sufferings of the rich man, since in this story the rich man's future is described as one of torment. We must ask, therefore, what the content and function of the story are. The answer must come from Lk. 16:19–26, independently of its context of faith in Jesus and, as is clear from what was said above, independently also of its literary context (Lk. 16:27–31 and the Gospel of Luke as a whole) and of parallels from the history of religions.

The positions taken by exegetes on the content and function of the story usually depend on whom the particular exegete considers the transmitting group and, above all, the addressees to have been. In E. Percy's view, the passage is a threat directed by Jesus at the rich.[71] H. Bolkestein gives a different interpretation: "It is clear that this version of the idea of retribution could arise and find adherents only among the poor for whom it represented the satisfaction of a sublimated need for revenge."[72] Gressmann has something similar in mind when he describes 16:10–25, taken as an isolated text, "submoral."[73] Others suggest that the text is addressed to dissatisfied disciples of Jesus who are scandalized by the prosperity of the wicked and the suffering of the devout and that its intention is to render them satisfied with their lot.[74]

It is possible, however, to avoid hypotheses regarding transmitting group and addressees and to determine function and content directly from the statements themselves. Luke 16:19–26 is not a warning to the rich, because in such an interpretation there is no real explanation of the role of Lazarus and because no alternative possible behavior of the rich man is specified. Nor is Lk. 16:19–26 an indictment of the rich, since their conduct is not described as sinful; the rich man is not depicted as guilty in regard to Lazarus. Nor, finally, does Lk. 16:19–26 express any desire for revenge upon the rich. The rich man suffers torment indeed, but Lazarus does not revel in his misery—and verse 26 has the function of explaining that he could not help the rich man, even if he wanted.

Luke 16:19–26 is built on a contrast: the luxury of the rich man in this life is set over against his torment in the next life; both the luxury and the torment are to be thought of as extreme. At the same time, the present distress and future happiness of the poor man are also clearly depicted and sharply contrasted. The contrasts are given further pictorial expression by the abyss that separates hell and Abraham's bosom in the next world (v. 26). The context makes the meaning of the abyss clear: it is the reflection in the next world of the gulf that separates rich and poor in this world, for this gulf too is wide and uncrossable. The sharpness of the contrasts in the story reflects the depth of the gulf between rich and poor in the present life. Its uncrossableness and the extreme opposition between rich and poor explain the future torment of the rich. The story specifies the hope of the poor, but without attacking the rich as guilty and without allowing the desire for revenge to enter the picture of their future in the next world. It expresses the hope that the poor have in a just God; Abraham speaks as God's representative. This hope is linked to the suffering caused by the impossibility of crossing the gulf between rich and poor.

7. The Magnificat (Lk. 1:46–54)

The Magnificat, too, must be located in the context of the earliest Jesus tradition. It is a pre-Lucan text, even in its present form (apart from minor stylistic revisions).[75] The Bible is used here to an even greater extent than in Lk. 6:20f. and Mt. 11:5 par. The Bible served the poor of that day as an aid in expressing themselves. With the help of the Bible they voiced their hopes and made it clear to themselves and others that their life, such as it was, was a disorder in God's sight. With the help of the Bible they could also give their hopes the greatest religious authority possible in their world. From the idea that God is Lord of Israel they drew conclusions that no one had hitherto drawn and that could not be acceptable to the influential groups in contemporary Judaism, since the concern of the poor was not with the future of Israel as a nation but with the correction of social inequity.

The mother of Jesus the Messiah is the lowly servant of God in whose destiny the destiny of all the lowly is symbolized. "Lowliness" (tapeinōsis) undoubtedly has a double meaning: low social status and humility before God. All future generations will praise Mary. Her exaltation represents the exaltation of all the lowly. The birth of Jesus the Messiah has already begun the great change. God's action will now bring about the comprehensive and definitive compensation. The psalmist speaks of this reversal as though it had already taken place: the mighty, who are also the arrogant, are cast down from their thrones; the rich lose their wealth; and the hungry and poor are filled with good things. In this poem the powerful and the rich lose only their power and their wealth; they are not punished in addition, but an end is put once and for all to their power and prosperity and arrogance.

The Magnificat permits us to infer that at a very early stage in the Jesus movement the birth of Jesus was itself understood as a saving action of God in behalf of Israel. The poem shows at what an early stage we have to allow for a distinct Christology. For those in the earliest Jesus movement, Jesus was not simply an equal among equals, but a human being who had changed the world:

God's Messiah who fulfills the divine promise given to Israel—and indeed to all of Israel (see especially Lk. 1: 54f.). The birth and preaching of Jesus mark the beginning of God's reign over Israel. It is not possible to say with certainty whether his death also already plays a part in this connection. In the later Palestinian Jesus movement, which reveals itself to us in the Sayings-source, his death is indeed significant, although not as a saving event.

The possibility cannot be excluded that even during his lifetime Jesus was revered as the Messiah (and that perhaps he also understood himself to be the Messiah); if so, it was as the Messiah of the poor whose destiny he shared, since there is no reason to doubt that he himself came from the stratum of the poor who belonged to the earliest Jesus movement. He was not a Messiah who effected the rule of Israel and its God over the rest of the world (on this point, see also below, chap. 2.II), but a Messiah who effected God's reign over Israel itself.

If we are to understand this movement and its vital religious manifestations, we must grasp the central importance of its hope: its expectation of God's reign. Here poor Jews come forward and claim that God's promises to Israel are now fulfilled and the misery of the present time—the distress of destitution—is ended. These people are no longer poor hungry cripples but a community of human beings who already experience in their fellowship what will soon come in its fullness: happiness, health, courage, hope. We may assume that they shared the little food they had; there is no textual proof of this, unless we claim Lk. 3:11 as evidence: "He who has two coats, let him share with him who has none; and he who has food, let him do likewise." (On Lk. 3:11, see also below, chap. 3.V.1).

8. Are There Extra-scriptural Analogies for the Hope of an Eschatological Reversal of Social Destinies?

Scholars have repeatedly suggested that even if the idea of an eschatological reversal be assumed to have existed in early Christianity, it was in any case not specifically Christian.[76] But, as we showed earlier, the analogy suggested by Gressmann for Lk. 16:19ff. did not involve an analogous content but was limited to comparable narrative motifs. As we also showed, the common ancient saying about the divinity's power to make the great little and the little great was indeed applied in numerous contexts, but in no instance was the content comparable to what we find in the Jesus tradition.

We turn now to further analogies that provide the best material for comparison with the eschatological hope of the poor in the earliest Jesus tradition. There are in fact a few texts that might be understood as referring to an eschatological hope of the poor for a reversal of their destiny.

The materials in question are these:

a) In the *Testaments of the Twelve Patriarchs* one textual tradition has the following addition in Judah 25, 4b: "And those who died in hunger will be filled; and those who died in weakness [sickness] will be made strong (Greek: "kai hoi en peinē chortasthesontai, kai hoi en astheneia ischysousin")." But there is much to suggest that this addition is a Christian interpolation.[77]

b) The Alphabetic Midrash of Rabbi Akiba offers a close parallel to Lk. 6:20f. (and its parallels in the New Testament): "The Holy One . . . looks at every moment solely upon the poor. . . . And the sound of their words is more pleasing to me than that of any of the children of men under heaven. . . . The Holy One . . . shows constant mercy to them and raises them from the dust; he gives them seats next to the noble ones, and they inherit the throne of glory, as it is written (1 Sam. 2:8)." An exegesis of 1 Sam. 2:8 follows, in which it is said, among other things, that "*kabod* (glory) refers only to the world that is coming. . . ."[78]

In this passage the eschatological exaltation of the poor is assumed, with poverty being understood solely as a condition of social distress. But as it continues, the text adopts a different position. The motif of eschatological reversal is now related to the following of the law: "Everyone who is poor in this world (is) rich in the world to come . . . as, for example, the Israelites, because they occupy themselves with the commandments. But those who are rich in this world are poor in the world to come, as, for example, the gentiles and sinners, who do not occupy themselves with the commandments."[79] Nor is the equation of Israel and the poor maintained; instead, the writer reflects on what will happen to a rich Israelite: If such a person acts rightly and therefore, among other good deeds, "gives alms to the poor and manifests love for the rich through loans," that person will enjoy "the fruits in this world, and the foundation will remain in the world to come."

This much is clear: the document shows that under the heading of "poverty" it is familiar with a tradition that promises the poor as such an exaltation in the world to come. The context does not, however, permit us to locate this tradition historically. It appears to be a tradition (early medieval?) that in its content is at odds with the views on poverty otherwise represented in rabbinical Judaism.[80]

c) Ethiopic Enoch 94–104 is frequently suggested as the primary analogy to Lk. 6:24–26. In fact, however, the cursing of the impious rich in this passage is not especially enlightening as a parallel either to Lk. 6:24ff. or to Lk. 6:20f., since the passage is not dealing with an apocalyptic reversal of social destinies.[81]

This section of Ethiopic Enoch presupposes a conflict that is seen through the eyes of the losers. Their distress is due primarily to their defeat in the conflict (see, e.g., 103, 9–15). That as a result they are also socially worse off than their adversaries is to be inferred from the fact that these adversaries are described as rich people (who have gained their wealth by injustice, 97, 8–10, etc.) and that the defeated are said not to have been provided for in their lifetime as their worth demanded (102, 5) and to have suffered the hardship of laborious toil (103, 9).

The losers in the conflict hope for a reward in heaven and for a final judgment (e.g., Ethiopian Enoch 104, 5) that will hand over those now powerful to those now defeated: "Do know that you will be given over into the hands of the righteous ones, and they shall cut off your necks and slay you, and they shall not have compassion on you" (98, 12). The primary aim of the passage is to hearten and exhort the "righteous" = the defeated: "Be hopeful, and do not abandon your hope" (104, 4); "Fear not . . . . do not be partners with them [sinners], but keep far away from those who lean on their own injustice" (104, 6). Theological differences also play a role in the conflict (e.g., 97, 4). In fact, it is very doubtful that the conflict can be regarded as a social one at all: the plight of the defeated is described not as one of social distress but as a political failure. And their hopes are directed not to social compensation but to victory over the adversary (despite 98, 3 and 104, 2: the passages that might most easily be interpreted as referring to an eschatological reversal of social destinies).

If we look back over the parallels discussed under a–c, we must conclude that Lk. 6:20f. (and related materials in the Jesus tradition) are not the product of a literary tradition, a religious tradition, or any other kind of tradition that might be included under the heading "history of ideas." A religious tradition is indeed presupposed, as the reference to Is. 61:1ff. shows, but this tradition is interpreted in a fully original way. Luke 6:20f. is not derivable from a religious or other history-of-ideas context.

There has been extensive discussion of the literary form (a macarism), but we need not go into this discussion here. It is clear that Lk. 6:20f. is not an ethical (sapiential)[82] but an apocalyptic macarism found probably on the lips of a prophet.[83] But the ascertainment of the literary form does not permit conclusions as to a particular life context (contrary to what is claimed by Koch).[84] Such inferences become permissible only after the content of the apocalyptic macarism has been determined; then the inference will be not to a life context in the community but to a life context of the community in the larger society.

9. Theological Uneasiness Regarding an Eschatological Reversal

Scholars have always been uneasy at the thought that the early Jesus movement could have cultivated this kind of hope: the hope that the reign of God would make the poor rich and the rich poor. Gressmann described Lk. 6:20f. as "submoral" and "primitive" and regarded the passage as pre-Christian. R. Bultmann expressed the uneasiness he felt at Lk. 6:20f. and 6:24ff. by saying that these texts could just as well have had a place in the final chapters of Ethiopic Enoch.[85] As a result, there have been many theological reinterpretations of the passages. Recourse has repeatedly been had to an ethicization of the concept "poor" in the Beatitude (poor = humble) or to the idea of the justification of the sinner (justificatio impii) (poor = poor in God's eyes). Some have doubted that the wording of Mk. 10:25 is correct (see above); others regard Mt. 20:16 as a proverb; and so on, and so on.

The hopes may indeed have been of a primitive kind; it was, after all, very poor people who joined Jesus or gathered in his name. And yet this hope contained such a vision of what human beings are created for that we may well envy these followers of Jesus their hope and the change it produced in their lives. It is really not valid to object, "But they starved anyway!" True, they did starve, but this is not an objection against the vision these people had—unless

we assume that because of their hope in the reign of God they blocked the way
to a new society. The objection presupposes possibilities that poor, helpless
human beings do not have; it is therefore cruel and illusory.

Despite Lk. 6:24f. and Lk. 16:19–26 the hope was not a hymn of revenge.
The positive perspective adopted made it unnecessary to humiliate the rich and
powerful or to treat them with cruelty; they had simply used up their portion of
happiness. Dreams of revenge have a different cast, as we can see from
Ethiopic Enoch. When faced with human wretchedness there are many ways of
denying its scandalous character. Even utopian visions of equality can do
injustice to still suffering human beings. Lucian, for example, has all human
beings equal in the kingdom of the dead: poor and rich are equal—equally
naked.

> Say (to the rich): Why do you guard your gold, you senseless fools? Why
> do you punish yourselves, counting interest, and piling talents on talents,
> when you must come here shortly with no more than a penny? . . .
> And tell the poor, my Spartan friend, who are many, displeased with
> life and pitying themselves for their poverty, not to cry and moan;
> describe to them our equality here, telling them how they'll see the rich on
> earth no better off here than they are themselves.[86]

Lucian's contempt for human beings may perhaps convince those who have
not yet overcome their distrust of the hope of the poor that is evidenced in the
earliest Jesus tradition. He adopts a point of view apart from the social realities
of rich and poor. In his *Dialogues of the Dead* the notion of the equality of all
human beings after death presupposes the uselessness of earthly effort. He has
no interest in balancing off the destinies of rich and poor. In face of death, the
great equalizer, all these things become utterly unimportant. Of course, only
someone who was not himself poor could adopt such an outlook.

Jesus, on the other hand, was the hope of the poor. Their wretched lives did
not become unimportant in the great perspective of the reign and kingdom of
God, but on the contrary were taken very seriously. To the extent that the poor
of the earliest Jesus tradition took seriously their future destiny (which had
already been inaugurated in Jesus) and regarded it as very real, they also had a
real and utterly consistent trust in the power of God. In their view the two were
directly connected.

IV. THE FRIEND OF TAX COLLECTORS AND SINNERS

If we are to understand the meaning of the friendship of Jesus with tax
collectors and sinners in the earliest Jesus tradition, we must not let our vision
be distorted by the emphatic development of this friendship in the Gospel of
Luke. The theme of the *metanoia* ("conversion") of tax collectors and sinners
is central to Luke's Gospel. A clear sign of this is the change found in Lk. 5:32
as compared with Mk. 2:17: according to Luke, Jesus came to call sinners to

repentance. The repentance of tax collectors and sinners is the central theological theme in Luke's description of the attitude of human beings before God. It must be said, however, that for Luke the idea of the acceptance of the sinner always has also a social reference: sinners in the social sense are given a welcome by God, and at the same time this makes it clear that God accepts all sinners.[87]

The theological interpretation of Jesus' association with tax collectors and sinners as oriented to their conversion is peculiar to the Gospel of Luke. If conversion was preached in the earliest Jesus movement, the call would hardly have been directed to the poor, tax collectors, and sinners, since their "sin" consisted in their wretched condition rather than any criminality. The call to conversion in the earliest Jesus movement would have been directed, rather, to the powerful in Israel. But this aspect of the earliest preaching can only be the subject of hypotheses.

A further peculiarity of Luke's treatment of Jesus' friendship with tax collectors and sinners is that among the tax collectors and sinners there were prosperous individuals as well as poor ones. Thus Zacchaeus, a chief tax collector, is rich (Lk. 19:1ff.); Levi the tax collector must also be thought of as well-off, since he has a house big enough for a "great feast" with a "large company" (as Lk. 5:29 elucidates the parallel passage in Mark, where it is not clear who precisely the host is). Similarly the prostitute in Lk. 7:36ff. does not clearly come from a wretched economic environment.[88]

All in all, we must not carry over the Lucan interpretation of Jesus' friendship with tax collectors and sinners into the texts of the earliest Jesus tradition. If we do, we shall fail to see the special character of the latter.[89]

In this context, three texts may be regarded as basic for the earliest Jesus tradition: Mt. 11:19,Q; Mt. 21:31; and Mk. 2:(13)14–17. The choice is dictated by traditio-historical reasons and similarity of content.

First, the traditio-historical arguments. The accusation (Mt. 11:19,Q) that Jesus is a friend of tax collectors and sinners is older even than the Sayings-source,[90] which sees the accusation as proof that Jesus has been rejected by an evil generation. There is no positive perspective in the way the Sayings-source treats this theme.

Matthew 21:31f. likewise contains older tradition. For Matthew the theme of the tax collectors and prostitutes is a means of representing the relationship between the Gentile Christians and the Jews. The Messiah had originally come to the Jews, but they rejected and killed him. The kingdom of God was therefore taken from them and given to those who do the Father's will (we need only read Mt. 21:43). The tax collectors and prostitutes exemplify the Gentile Christians: one would not expect them to do the Father's will, and yet they have done it and are now privileged over the Jews. Since the pairing of tax collectors and prostitutes obviously no longer has any concrete social meaning for Matthew, we may judge Mt. 21:31 to be of pre-Matthean origin.

Even more may the story of the tax collector's banquet in Mk. 2:14–17 be claimed for the earliest tradition about Jesus, not as a historical record but as an "ideal scene," which in its substance accurately reflects the historical situation. Mark himself has but a secondary interest in the scene: his aim is, on the one hand, to show the origin of the deadly enmity of the Pharisees and, on the other, the authority of the Son of man to forgive the sins of sinners (see Mk. 2:10). But in 2:14–17 (pre-Marcan) the Pharisees are not irreconcilable enemies of Jesus, and the tax collectors and sinners do not exemplify all sinners but are only a special group of human beings in a special social condition. From the traditio-historical standpoint, therefore, the same judgment applies to Mk. 2:14–17 as to Mk. 2:23–27, where the story of the plucking of the ears of grain on the sabbath is likewise pre-Marcan.

If we compare these basic texts of the earliest Jesus tradition they show a striking similarity of content. All three reflect a conflict between the Jesus movement and some other Jews on account of the tax collectors and sinners.

In Mt. 21:31 there is a sharp attack on these other Jews: "The tax collectors and harlots go into the kingdom of God before you." It cannot be said with certainty whether this means "they go in first, and then you," or "they go in and not you." The language as such allows both interpretations. The exclusive meaning is linguistically improbable but nonetheless possible.[91]

But a position on this point does not play a decisive part in the interpretation, since by any accounting the text shows a sharp attack being made. The depiction of the future destiny of the addressees may well be derived, by way of analogy, from the tradition about the eschatological reversal of social destinies. In that tradition, too, there is no strictly logical representation of the destiny of the rich in the kingdom of God: they will be the "last," they will experience hunger, they will go away empty, or they will even be unable to enter the kingdom at all (Mk. 10:25). The important point is that in this life they have already used up their portion of happiness. So too, whether Mt. 21:31 be interpreted as exclusive or as showing a temporal succession, the result is not a real alternative; in either case the meaning is that the adversaries no longer have any right to make claims for themselves.

We may think that the addressees in Mt. 21:31 are precisely those Jews who deny tax collectors and prostitutes the right to hope in God. It does not automatically follow, however, that these adversaries are the Pharisees. Two considerations bar such a conclusion: the closeness of the first-century Pharisees to the ordinary people and the scantiness of traditions regarding a specific hostility of the Pharisees toward tax collectors.[92]

A further point: the association of tax collectors and prostitutes is so concrete as to exclude the possibility of understanding Mt. 21:31 in a figurative sense and thus of interpreting it, for example, as a statement about the position before God of "sinners" in a consciously theological sense of this term. Mt. 21:31 means simply: the wretched prostitutes and customhouse employees, scorned by every educated and refined person, are preferred by God to their despisers. If we wish, we may put it more graphically: they will put your noses out of joint! The statement is remarkably clear.

Mark 2:14–17 likewise shows that the association of Jesus' followers with tax collectors and sinners could lead to conflict. But, once again, the passage should not be interpreted as meaning that the Pharisees were in a special way the enemies of tax collectors, sinners, and their friends. In fact the Pharisees show themselves here in a much more serious and reflective mood. They ask why Jesus does not avoid tax collectors and sinners, and, on hearing of their question, he gives them a serious theological answer, which should enable them to understand his friendship with sinners: "Those who are well have no need of a physician, but those who are sick. I came not to call the righteous, but sinners" (Mk. 2:17).

Jesus is here already the one who invites human beings to the banquet in the kingdom of God (no ordinary host!). This interpretation of him is to be found everywhere in the earliest tradition. The present passage speaks of tax collectors and sinners as "sick" and as "sinners," that is, sinners not only in the eyes of their fellow human beings but in the eyes of God as well. That "sinners" has this theological meaning here is clear from the contrast between "righteous" and "sinners"; Jesus is using theological categories. But that God has mercy on sinners was also a major theme in the theology of the Pharisees,[93] and Jesus addresses them in that light: "You yourselves say that God is just *and* merciful; he has mercy on sinners." The only thing surprising to the Pharisees is that "sinners" should take concrete form in these tax collectors and criminals.

At the level of theological reflection, then, the Pharisees would accept what is said in Mk. 2:17 (apart from its Christological implications); they would not, however, accept its concrete interpretation by the Jesus movement. As theologians they thought of God primarily as the one before whom no human being can claim to be without sin. Here, then, as in Mk. 2:27 an appeal is made to them on the basis of their own theology.[94] The disciples of Jesus do not reject them and their question, but seek to win them over. In the time of the earliest Jesus movement the Pharisees are not yet the representatives of a Judaism that is hostile to Christianity; they are not the adversaries of Jesus but, rather, participants in a discussion within Judaism. The followers of Jesus can deal seriously with them and can evidently expect them to understand the path these followers have chosen and perhaps even to approve their religious claims.

The same picture of the relationship between the earliest Jesus movement and Pharisaism emerges from Mk. 2:23-27. It is a historically probable picture, inasmuch as the Pharisees were not yet the leaders of Judaism and, like the Jesus movement, though in a different way, were attempting to deal theologically with Israel's present distress. Another argument for the historical probability of the picture is that the bitter polemical attitude to the Pharisees emerges only in the late strata of the synoptic tradition.[95] This no longer realistic negative picture of the Pharisees should not be projected back into Palestine and the earliest Jesus movement. The earliest Jesus movement justified itself by the law (see Mk. 2:25) and made a positive appeal to the faith of the Pharisees (Mk. 2:27, 17).

The fact that Jesus is described as "friend" of tax collectors and sinners (Mt. 11:19, Q) confirms the picture given in the passages just analyzed. That is, the accusation confirms the solidarity of the followers of Jesus with tax collectors and sinners; in the society of the time such solidarity was expressed by sharing the same table. The accusation is also confirmation of the conflict that arose because of the solidarity.

What kind of historical picture can we paint of what happened in the earliest Jesus movement? The supporters of the movement were poor Jews. They included tax collectors, sinners, and prostitutes. The solidarity among these people—a solidarity symbolized by Jesus and probably originating in him—did not cease when one of their number proved to have been guilty of offenses in his or her wretched life. We must not think of the friendship with tax collectors and sinners as an external demonstration whereby Jesus and his followers tried to make the powerful (or even the Pharisees) aware of the injustice they were committing. In the beginning at least, there was no question of such a demonstration. That sort of thing would not have been a source of hope for the tax collectors and sinners. Nor could the followers of Jesus have enhanced the status of these people by association; such an enhancement would not have changed in any way the wretched condition of a tax-office employee.[96]

There was no question of a demonstration to others, but rather, a real association of human beings whose living conditions put them in a hopeless situation—whether they were simply poor or were tax collectors in addition. Their association enabled them to cope with their lives and filled them with hope in God, in whose eyes they were not "last" but "first." In adopting this outlook the Jesus movement was making an enormous religious claim. It was asserting that God is on the side of those worst off in the present world. It was claiming that God takes the part of the poor and the tax collectors, simply because they are poor, deprived and despised. And consequently it was claiming also that the God of Israel was now inaugurating the reign for which many Jews of the day were longing—but inaugurating it among these lowly and despised folk. No greater religious claim could have been made in the context of the Jewish religion. This claim was the cause of the attacks on the Jesus movement.

The adversaries of the followers of Jesus attacked them because there were tax collectors and sinners among them. They contemptuously described Jesus as a friend of tax collectors and sinners and sought thereby to compromise him and his followers religiously. From a social standpoint it was hardly possible to compromise further this group of poor people and tax collectors, since they were already at the bottom of the social heap, down there in their slums. It was still possible, however, to render implausible their enormous religious claim.

As a result of this conflict, once the followers of Jesus refused to dissociate themselves from tax collectors and sinners, their solidarity with such people did take on the aspect of a demonstration aimed at outsiders. But why did the followers of Jesus accept tax collectors and sinners among them? Why did they not dissociate themselves from them?

This question, which the Pharisees ask in Mk. 2:16, is precisely the question that has to be asked. Where do we find a religious movement, a group making a religious claim, that does not lay down conditions? That does not require, for example, a certain profession of beliefs or a certain kind of behavior? Where do we find a group that is defined by a religious claim and that does not understand itself in an exclusive way, for example, as a holy remnant, which amid the mass of the wicked holds high the banner of truth? And yet the followers of Jesus evidently rejected any and all exclusivity and were attacked for this reason. Precisely such a nonexclusivity is shown by the tradition of Jesus' association with tax collectors and sinners.[97] The followers of Jesus claimed, on the one hand, that the reign of God was beginning. They claimed, on the other hand, that in the kingdom of God the poor would no longer get the short end of the stick, and they did not attempt to protect their lofty religious claim by introducing any exclusivity. This was a characteristic of the Jesus movement, which in this respect maintained a high degree of continuity, since in the Sayings-source the understanding of love of enemies shows the same structure.

Why did the followers of Jesus refuse to protect their religious claims by practicing exclusivity? Although the texts give no explicit response, the answer is to be found in their expectation of God's reign, in their idea of God. The idea that God reigns was universally accepted in Israel; this was the God in whom every Israelite believed. God had made promises to Israel. Now, in the middle of the first century A.D., in a time of terrible misery and destitution, poor Jews formed an association with tax collectors and sinners in Israel and claimed this Israel for its God. Good news was at last preached to the poor: God's promise was now being fulfilled for them. If it meant anything at all to say that God was the God of *all* Israel, it meant that *now* the poor were given preference. God's claim to a universal kingship was not explicitly stated, but it was already present in the words "God reigns." The Jesus movement can be understood and explained only in light of an understanding of God that was shared with the Old Testament and Judaism.

God was therefore the God also of the Jewish enemies of Jesus' followers—even in the eyes of these followers. God was also the God of the rich—even in the eyes of the poor. But if it was true that God is the Lord of all, then God's promise must be fulfilled first in those whose actual existence was most remote from that promise of a life free from want and suffering. Blessed are the poor. The tax collectors and sinners will enter the kingdom of God before you.

In the next two chapters we shall try to answer the question: What happened subsequently to the Jesus movement? We shall focus our attention on two important sources: the Sayings-source and the Gospel of Luke. But as we attempt to grasp the historical characteristics of the various stages in the story of discipleship, we must not be too quick to ask about continuity or discontinuity in the history of this discipleship. The first need is to analyze the historical characteristics that the discipleship displayed in a given place and at a given time.

2

Sheep among Wolves: The Wandering Prophets
of the Sayings-source

The Sayings-source has long been the object of historical study; until now, however, it has rarely elicited theological interest. A discussion of it provides an important opportunity for clarifying basic theological choices despite the fact that the group represented by this source lives what is at first sight a very strange life. The people behind the Sayings-source are wandering preachers of a proximate end of the world, and their manner of life and their message regarding Jesus produce central texts on questions regarding property. "Where your treasure is, there will your heart be also" (Mt. 6:19-21,Q);[1] "You cannot serve God and mammon" (Mt. 6: 23,Q); "Give us our bread this day" (Mt. 6:11,Q); and "Do not be anxious about your life, what you shall eat . . . " (Mt. 6:25-33,Q).

The Sayings-source makes clear both the social location of the source itself and the context of the message about Jesus that these wandering preachers proclaim. The other contents of this message are materially closely connected with the outlook on property. Rejection of the service of mammon, love of enemies, proclamation of judgment against the destroyers of hope, and the idea that God is Father and Creator and that by the coming of Jesus the world has been changed for the better—these themes are closely connected in the Sayings-source.

As we saw earlier, the Sayings-source in its turn transmits older tradition about Jesus. In this context mention must be made in particular of the Beatitude of the poor, which originally belonged in an earlier context of the following of Jesus and which the Sayings-source appropriates and actualizes in its own way by adding the Beatitude of the persecuted disciples (Mt. 5:11f.,Q). The disciples are now the poor whom Jesus calls blessed. It is no longer possible to determine whether the texts cited above on the attitude to property likewise have earlier tradition (prior to Q) behind them.

"Sayings-source" (Q) is understood here as a written collection of preachers' sayings, which Matthew and Luke knew, directly or indirectly, and which they made use of in addition to using Mark. In our opinion, the method we have adopted in dealing with this source is a reliable one. It is to regard as components of the Sayings-source those texts that show such material agreement in their transmission in Matthew and Luke that this very agreement already makes a clear statement. In these cases it is permissible to ignore stylistic discrepancies between Matthew and Luke as well as theological interventions by Matthew and Luke that are easily recognizable and beyond doubt.

An example of this kind of relatively unchallenged reconstruction of Q is Mt. 6:25-33,Q. In the case of parallel traditions in Matthew and Luke, for which it is more difficult to establish the form in Q, and, above all, in the case of traditions peculiar to Matthew and Luke, which scholars would like to claim for Q, it is necessary first to establish that their content belongs in the Sayings-source. For example: although from the standpoints of literary history and tradition history Lk. 6:24-26 could have been part of Q, this condemnation of the rich will not be used here in reconstructing the preaching in Q inasmuch as the announcement of judgment against the rich could hardly have had its original setting in Q (any more than could the Beatitude of the poor). Why? Because the idea of an eschatological reversal is used only secondarily in Q and is not part of its central content.

Our purpose here, then, is not to provide a complete literary picture of Q but, rather, to discuss focal points in the preaching of a particular group of Jesus' followers, points that, despite the complicated transmission, combine to form a clear picture. For, surprising as it may sound, a clear and very distinctive picture of a preaching about Jesus does emerge from the sum-total of texts that definitely belong to the Sayings-source. We assume that the Sayings-source had a literary prehistory and, more important, a literary posthistory (e.g., in the form of a "redaction") until the time when Matthew and Luke made use of it. Our concern here, however, is not to show the literary destiny of the Sayings-source but to come to grips with its central contents. As the mutual material relations of these contents show, they point essentially to a single originating situation—or, if in fact they came from an earlier time, they acquired a new significance when placed in the new context of the life and preaching reflected in the Sayings-source.

I. TRUST IN GOD AS A WAY OF LIFE

1. The Sayings-source and the Anxieties of the Ordinary People

The Sayings-source gives expression to the anxieties of the ordinary people. There are two ways of showing this to be the case. The first is to attempt to locate the Q passage on "anxieties" (worries, cares) in the real-life context that emerges more or less clearly in Mt. 20:1-16. The second is then to test the results in light of the train of thought in the passage itself (in other words, to test it exegetically).

It is 9 A.M. in the marketplace of a small town in Galilee. A farm worker is standing there with a group of his fellows. They are waiting for work, although there's now really nothing to expect, since the farmers come early in the morning to hire helpers for the day. The farm worker broods: "What shall we eat? True enough, grain or even baked bread is dearer in Jerusalem than here in this little town, but we can't pay for it in any case if I do not earn anything today. What are we to drink? For some months now even water has cost money, ever since the good well dried up! What shall we wear? As it is, all we have is rags, but the last remnant of self-respect will disappear if we can't dress neatly even on the sabbath. In any case, clothing is absurdly expensive. In this season it will take only three days without work for my family to be in great trouble. Hunger already has its grip on us, and there is no escaping it. And if you get undernourished you're soon so weak and in such bad condition that you can no longer work. The few alms you're lucky enough to pick up suffice only for a life as a half-sick vagabond."

In light of what we know of the life of the many farm workers (and small farmers) in the first-century Palestine, this imaginative version of the setting in Mt. 20:1-16 accurately reflects the real situation. In general, the parable of the workers in the vineyard (Mt. 20:1-16) and the parable of the rascally servant (Mt. 18:23-35) may be regarded as descriptions of actual conditions in Palestine. The *doulos* (slave, servant) of Mt. 18:23-35 who owes 100 denarii is not yet a slave in the legal sense; he is a dependent farmer who is already so much in debt that slavery lies only a step away for himself and his family. The *ergates* (worker) in Mt. 20:1-16 is a day laborer who can envy even slaves. The slaves who belong on the farm at least need not suffer constant anxiety about their daily bread; they are not so constantly threatened with the loss of the minimum needed for life. Only if they fall sick or get old will they be put out on the street. Matthew 20:1-16 and Mt. 18:23-35 (that is, the pictorial material of these parables) depict the social situation of the people who work on the land, and therefore of an important sector of the population.[2]

The few big landowners and rich farmers likewise had their worries, though they would hardly have recognized them in the anxieties of Mt. 6:25-33,Q. The care that turns the rich into insomniacs was in fact proverbial in antiquity: they worry that thieves may steal their money, that lazy workers may ruin them, that their stores of grain may go bad.[3] Philosophical circles advised the rich to adopt the simple life with its freedom from cares: human beings really do not need sumptuous clothing and sophisticated foods; simple dress, some grain, beans, and pure water are enough for a happy life. Follow the example of the great men: Socrates or Diogenes of Sinope or Crates![4]

Many of the rich were grateful to the preachers of morality. They attempted to take a more relaxed attitude to their possessions and their cares. Indeed, ardent young men from well-to-do families even came to think, "Should we not live like Socrates and Diogenes? Really, and not just intellectually, as our parents do?" But after the first night in the open the heroic decision was forgotten. They suddenly realized that the magnanimous decision could have troublesome consequences: sickness, starvation. Epictetus derides such young men: You will shiver? You may lack the bare minimum for survival? Yet you know that at worst the road leads to death. Take as your model runaway slaves who live from hand to mouth and have no homes. Are you more cowardly than runaway slaves? "Then you fear starvation, as you think; but what you really fear is not starvation; you are afraid that you may not have a cook, that you may not have another to cater for you, to shoe you, another to dress you."[5]

It was easy for Epictetus to talk; after all, it was only as an observer that he knew the life of the runaway slaves and beggars of whom he was speaking. The young men who shrank from the simple life as really a state of emergency were quite right. The voluntary adoption of a vagabond simple life was a risky thing, and only rarely did well-to-do individuals go so far. Far more often they simply enthused over the simple life while continuing to live in their fine houses. People of some education thought this the thing to do.

Those who developed a bad conscience because of the gap between theory and practice might take in a dirty, bearded wandering philosopher and give him a bowl of soup and a bed. Of course, they might well think their guest to be telling outright lies about having nobly renounced his possessions when he abandoned family and home. And in fact many of the unemployed, former craftsmen and day laborers who "could hardly earn their daily bread despite all their hard toil," slipped into the guise of wandering philosophers, in the hope that by begging they might live better than before.[6]

The rich, then, continued their worry-filled lives—unless they learned to handle their possessions and cares with composure and an inner detachment and thereby found, at least in their interior attitude, the freedom from care that went with the simple life.

The anxieties of day laborers (or small farmers) and the anxieties of the rich were not the same, because day laborers had to worry about the minimum needed for survival. It is of this basic concern that Mt. 6:25-33,Q speaks. We cannot exaggerate the extent of the anxiety about daily survival at this period; as the few words cited above from Lucian show, this anxiety was not limited to Palestine. A. Ben-David has calculated that in Palestine

> 200 denarii, the minimum for survival in the period of the Mishnah, could buy 2400 loaves of bread. A farm worker's daily wage of a denarius could thus buy 12 loaves of bread and, since he could work about 200 days a year, his earning amounted to the minimum for survival. In the case of a family of six the minimal income of 200 denarii would buy 400 loaves of bread a year for each person or, in other words, 1400 calories a day. A caloric intake this low barely supplies the minimum nutritional needs of a human being.[7]

The consciousness of living with the bare minimum for survival also finds expression in this rabbinical saying: "Those who have bread in their baskets today and say: What will I eat tomorrow? are simply fainthearted."[8]

The link between the Sayings-source and the life of the ordinary people can be observed elsewhere too, and not just in Mt. 6:25-33,Q. The distance that separated the day laborer from the rich is shown indirectly in a Q saying on the relationship between the Jewish populace and the Baptist: "What did you go out to see? A man clad in fine garments? Behold, they who wear fine garments are in the houses of kings!" (Mt. 11:8,Q).[9] Of course you were not so absurd as to think you could gape at a rich man in the wilderness; it was a prophet you wanted to see. Even the choice of images in the Sayings-source reflects the social reality of the ordinary people: God forgives debts (Mt. 6:12,Q). And the little scene in Mt. 5:23f.,Q (whose theological relevance for Q is no longer clear) depicts an everyday occurrence in the lives of these same people: "Be submissive to him who intends to accuse you, and be quick about it, while you are still on the road with him, so that he may not hand you over to the judge, and the judge to the bailiff, and you be thrown into prison. Amen, I tell you, you will not come out from there until you have paid the last penny."[10]

Social historians at times complain, and with justice, that the ancient sources tell us so little about the life and, above all, the cares of the majority of the population: the poor, slaves, rural workers, and farmers.[11] Given this limitation of the sources in question, the synoptic Gospels evidently prove to be a historical document of rare value, since the materials in particular that come from the Sayings-source and the earliest Jesus tradition reflect the everyday experiences of the ordinary people, who are for the most part overlooked in historical writing.

2. The Exhortation to Freedom from Anxiety and Fear (Mt. 6:25-33,Q; 10:28-31,Q)

It is important, if we are to understand Mt. 6:25-33,Q, that we realize the social gulf separating us from the passages. As the history of exegesis shows, the affluence enjoyed by interpreters often causes them to see the texts of the Jesus tradition as less concrete than they were intended to be. Then the anxiety or care in Mt. 6:25-33,Q becomes anxiety or care in one or other figurative sense. It becomes, for example, the worry that even well-to-do Western Christians feel when they think of their own future or that of their children. Even a Bultmannian existential interpretation of the texts of the Jesus tradition is a hermeneutical approach that turns concrete social relations into abstractions, which can then be concretized in new ways. Bultmann interprets the "care" of Mt. 6:25-33,Q as "meta-care": "Every man naturally cares for himself and his life. . . . He is concerned about himself. . . . He is always intent on something and concerned about something."[12] The concrete form given to this abstraction is no longer necessarily the undisguised anxiety about the minimum for survival of which the Q passage is speaking.

We have thus far used primarily the juxtaposition of social reality and text to show that the anxiety of the ordinary people is the theme of this central text of the Sayings-source. But we can reach the same conclusion exegetically, especially if we look at the exhortation to freedom from care in its *literary* context, the Sayings-source. The exhortation here closely matches the exhortation to freedom from anxiety in time of persecution. The two texts have numerous points in common.

Matthew 10:28-31, Q:

And do not fear those who kill the body (*soma*) but cannot kill the soul (*psyche*); rather fear him who can destroy both soul and body in hell. Are not two sparrows sold for a penny? And not one of them will fall to the ground without your Father's will. But even the hairs of your head are all numbered. Fear not, therefore; you are of more value than many sparrows.

Matthew 6:25-33, Q:

Therefore I tell you, do not be anxious about your soul (*psyche*), what you shall eat or what you shall drink, nor about your body (*soma*), what you shall put on. Is not the soul more than food, and the body more than clothing?

Look at the birds of the air: they neither sow nor reap nor gather into barns, and yet your heavenly Father feeds them. Are you not of more value than they?

And which of you by being anxious can add one cubit to your span of life?

And why are you anxious about clothing? Consider the lilies of the field, how they grow; they neither toil nor spin; yet I tell you, even Solomon in all his glory was not arrayed like one of these.

But if God so clothes the grass of the field, which today is alive and tomorrow is thrown into the oven, will he not much more clothe you, O people of little faith? Therefore do not be anxious, saying, "What shall we eat?" or "What shall we drink?" or "What shall we wear?" For the Gentiles seek all these things; and your heavenly Father knows that you need them all. But seek first God's kingdom and God's righteousness, and all these things shall be yours as well.[13]

Both exhortations prove God's providence with an argument from nature to human being (*a minore ad maius*, from the lesser to the greater).

Sparrows (the cheapest edible birds, and the poor person's roast[14]), the hairs on one's head, the birds of heaven, the lilies of the field (or the grass)—all these demonstrate that God exercises a providential care in even the littlest part of the natural world, no matter how small and transient the living thing in question be.

Nature here is often erroneously understood as an exemplar for the behavior being required. This interpretation is connected with the fact that such an argument is often used in the moral philosophy of antiquity: for example, the ants are taken as a model of diligence (Prov. 6:6ff). In general, the texts we are discussing do show a familiarity with literary motifs from the

writings of antiquity. On the other hand, the motifs are used in a very uncon-
ventional way. Compare, for example, the motif in Mt. 6:29f.,Q (on Solomon's
splendor) with the following parallel: "The tale is told by some that Croesus sat
himself on his throne in full regalia and asked him [Solon], whether he had ever
seen a finer spectacle. 'Yes,' was the reply, 'cocks and pheasants and peacocks;
for they shine in nature's colours, which are ten thousand times more beauti-
ful.' "[15]

The intention in Mt. 6:29f.,Q is to show that God cares for human beings,
since God adorns even the flowers so wonderfully that their splendor outshines
Solomon's. The intention in the scene with Croesus and Solon is to show that
nature is superior to artificial luxury. The authors of the scriptural exhortations to freedom from worry and fear undoubtedly had some degree of literary
formation, but they put these tag ends of an education at the service of quite
original ideas, so that (as here in the Solomon/Croesus motif) the thought
becomes somewhat distorted. In Mt. 6:29,Q a critique of luxury is a superflu-
ous addition that is suggested by the literary motif. The point to which the train
of thought is moving is in verse 30.

Both of the Q texts make use of the soul-body anthropology. In each instance
the thought is entirely and independently clear: The power of human beings to
kill you is small compared to the power of God, since they do not have power
over the entire person; only God has that (Mt. 10:28,Q). Matthew 6:25,Q says
the same thing as Mt. 4:4,Q (Deut. 8:3b): "Man shall not live by bread alone."
"Do not be anxious about your soul, what you shall eat" should be read as a
parallel (a synonymous, not a synthetic parallel) of the next words ("nor about
your body, what you shall put on"). Soul and body each stand for the whole
person as a part for the whole. The point is that a human being is more than
food and clothing. When judged by ancient applications, the use of the body-
soul anthropology here gives rise to an absurdity: the linking of *soma* and
clothing in Mt. 6:25,Q, and the enigmatic illogicality of Mt. 10:28,Q (Does the
body die at death or does it not?).[16]

It is clear that the exhortations to freedom from anxiety and fear belong
closely together. In the sight of God human beings are more than their death or
their hunger and thirst. Just as a possible martyr's death is not meant in a
metaphorical sense, neither is the anxiety about food and clothing. In both
cases the threats are real: the addressees must accept the possibility of a
martyr's death, and they are beset by anxiety about the minimum for survival.

What do the exhortations offer that will offset terror and misery? The
exhortations call for an attitude of limitless trust in God's power and providential care. Fear of God and trust in God are one and the same thing. It is God
who decides how long a life you are to live (Mt. 6:27,Q); if you die a martyr's
death, that is God's will (Mt. 10:29–31,Q), since not even a sparrow dies
without God's decreeing it. You must see yourselves as human beings who
stand in God's presence and are therefore more than the wretched needs that
attack you. The danger is not denied. The text does not say, "Nothing will
happen to you"; no, the threat is a real threat. It says, rather, "Do not
succumb; do not become mere subjects of distress that makes you anxious and

helpless." There can be no more radical version of liberation from distress (a martyr's death, and anxiety about the minimum for survival) than to say, "Human beings do not live by bread alone; human beings are more than their death; human beings are more than food and clothing." At this point we ask hesitantly, "Was this liberation purely in the mind? A complete illusion?" (Many interpretations of the passages give that impression; e.g., Bultmann, *TDNT* 4:592: "Everything as before, but without anxiety.")

The followers of Jesus who are reflected in the Sayings-source attempted to live their daily lives with this kind of trust in God. This is especially clear in the case of the wandering messengers of Jesus, whose way of life emerges clearly from the missionary discourse according to Q. But even sedentary followers of Jesus lived according to the demands of the Sayings-source, as we shall see.

3. The Missionary Discourse in the Sayings-source [17]

> The harvest is plentiful, but the laborers (*ergatai*) are few; pray therefore the Lord of the harvest to send out laborers into his vineyard [Mt. 9:37f.,Q→ Lk. 10:2b].

The harvest is a metaphor for the reign of God; the work of the messengers is their prophetic task. We may ask whether it is simply an accident that the images used in the metaphor are in contrast to the social reality of the time. That is, at that time many workers (*ergatai*) were without work, and the harvest was rarely felt to be plentiful, since food was so hard to come by. Consequently the saying just cited must have seemed to mean: "Here you will be used."

> Behold, I send you out as sheep in the midst of wolves [Mt. 10:16a,Q→ Lk. 10:3].

The meaning is: you are in danger and defenseless. Perhaps both the originators and the addressees of the saying were also conscious that the metaphor of the sheep among wolves was elsewhere occasionally used to describe Israel's existence among the nations. Now Israelites were suddenly the wolves,[18] as the proclamation of judgment shows (see below). In the Sayings-source, defenselessness is part of the practice of love of enemies (on this point, see below).

> Take no gold, nor silver, nor copper in your belts, no bag for your journey, nor two tunics, nor sandals, nor a staff [Mt. 10:9-10,Q→ Lk. 10:4; see also Lk. 9:3; 22:35; Mk. 6:8f.].

The messengers have no money and therefore cannot buy food. They have no bag for supplies and therefore cannot store food but are faced with daily uncertainty about how they are to live. They have brought no second undergarment (*chiton = tunica*) on their wanderings, although even the poorest try to have a second clean undergarment; an outer garment, that also served as a cover for sleeping, was usually too expensive for poor people.[19] They have no shoes, which makes walking arduous and dangerous on the stony and difficult roads; even beggars try to have sandals, however broken. They lack even a staff for defense against animals. It is not possible to be less equipped than this; there is nothing more to discard. A reasonably well-prepared traveler would take all these things along, while a beggar would have to have lost his last will to survive before doing without staff, bag, and sandals.

From the standpoint of method it is important to see that we shall not be helped in understanding this lack of basic articles by searching through the history of motifs (e.g., going barefoot signals moderation of one's needs in Pseudo-Lucian's dialogue *Cynicus*. May that possibly be the meaning here?).[20] The interpretation must focus, rather, on the set of rules for equipment in their entirety and look within the Sayings-source for reasons that explain their content.

The lack of equipment is explained by the exhortation against anxiety (Mt. 6:25-33,Q): there is no more contention for food or drink or clothing. The only thing added here is renunciation of anxiety about where one is to sleep at night. This is the special problem of people who are itinerant, and is not faced in Mt. 6:25-33,Q.

The rule about equipment signifies that these people no longer yield to anxiety about the minimum needed for survival, but commit themselves with (literally) empty hands and bare feet to the providential care of God, while being fully aware of the dangers they are accepting (see the metaphor of the sheep among wolves and the consciousness of danger in Mt. 10:28-31,Q; Mt. 6:25-33,Q; etc.).

But if we are really to understand this lack of preparedness, we must locate the renunciation of anxiety about the minimum for survival in the context of contemporary social reality. The majority of the population were involved in a struggle for the necessary minimum, and knew how easily the struggle could be lost. The poverty of the wandering messengers of Jesus differed only in very small ways from that of their (still) sedentary friends and from the lives of other no longer sedentary people: the unemployed and the beggars. The messengers of Jesus voluntarily placed themselves on the bottom rung of the social ladder. Seen from the sociological standpoint, that is, externally and without regard for the intention the messengers themselves had, these wanderers were part of the great movement of flight for social reasons, a movement that can be documented for almost all the societies of antiquity.[21] Flight for social reasons is depicted in Lucian's dialogue *Fugitivi*, but also in Job: "They thrust the poor off the road; the poor of the earth all hide themselves. /Behold, like wild asses in the desert they go forth to their toil, seeking prey in the wilderness as food for their children" (Job 24:4-5).

This passage to a wandering life on the part of the messengers of Jesus should not be called a "renunciation of possessions." It was, rather, an attempt to rid themselves of the oppressive anxiety about the minimum for survival by trusting to the providential care of God. It took courage to liberate themselves in this way from their anxiety. The messengers saw their action as an alternative to enslavement by poverty, and they traveled the land as living proofs of trust in God's care. God takes care of the animals and plants; you are a human being, a creature of God whom hunger and death cannot destroy; if you go under in the process, that is God's will.

Matthew 6:25–33,Q, the rule about equipment, and the part played by anxiety about the minimum for survival in broad sectors of the population—all these must be seen as interconnected. Matthew 6:25–33,Q is not describing the special existence of the wandering messengers of Jesus as contrasted with that of sedentary Christians; nor was anxiety about the minimum for survival a special problem of Christians. The renunciation of preparedness is an implementation of Mt. 6:25–33,Q; it was no less possible for (still) sedentary Christians to obey the exhortation in that passage and to set aside their anxiety.

A comparison with an earnest Cynic philosopher[22] will help us to appreciate better the substantive uniqueness of the quest for liberation. *Cynicus,* a dialogue of Pseudo-Lucian, describes a wandering philosopher who lives in a manner very like that of the wandering prophets of the Sayings-source: barefooted, with a minimum of clothing, itinerant, living like a beggar from hand to mouth. His appearance and manner are meant to demonstrate that a life characterized by very modest needs is an alternative to the life of the rich. The Cynic's moderation finds an exemplar in the animals. His message is addressed to the rich. The latter are insatiable gluttons who grab the biggest dishes for themselves at God's banquet (i.e., life). "You resemble very closely that man who snatches up everything in his uncontrolled greed. . . . The gold for which you pray, the silver, the expensive houses . . . consider how much they cost in trouble, in toil, in danger, or rather in blood, death, and destruction for mankind."[23]

The philosopher is not worried that people may mistake him for a genuine beggar. The important thing to him is that he not be identified with the affluent. He has chosen this life freely and deprived himself voluntarily of prosperity.

Here a man formerly well-to-do is showing his own class the alternative to a life of luxury and to the exploitation of dependents, which luxury always presupposes. Although the passage puts little emphasis on a renunciation of property by the Cynic, that step must be regarded as self-evident in the case of such a person. The choice of this kind of life was certainly the exception, something rarely found in practice. In any case the choice represents an impressive attempt at an alternative life, or at least an alternative to the luxurious life of the rich. The prophets of the Sayings-source likewise sought an alternative, but an alternative to the life of the ordinary people with its oppressive anxiety about daily survival.

It becomes necessary at this point to discuss two very important interpretations of the wandering prophets of the Sayings-source: those of Poul Hoffman and Gerd Theissen. We must indicate the points on which we agree with their interpretations and those on which we think a different view must be taken.

Excursus: "Vagabond Radicalism" as Interpreted by Poul Hoffman and Gerd Theissen

We are essentially in agreement with Hoffman in his interpretation of the rule regarding equipment.[24] He correctly sees a connection between the appearance on the scene of the messengers of Jesus, and the social reality of poverty and the use of violence. He also understands the renunciation of basic equipment and the exhortation not to be anxious as a manifestation of trust in God and an effort to show others how one can "deal with" the reality of poverty and violence. He does not see, however, that anxiety about the minimum for survival is the lot of many human beings and that Mt. 6:25-33,Q has this in view. Therefore he understands the coming of the messengers in demonstrative poverty to be a consequence of a renunciation of possessions and an act of deliberate defenselessness (intended to counter the Zealots).[25] This picture of the messengers brings them closer to the Cynic who was presenting a living alternative to the lives of the rich and was addressing his message to them.

It is not at all clear in what the alternative to the life of the lowly consists if the messengers come on the scene in a poverty intended as a demonstration. In fact, they emerge not in demonstrative poverty—they and their clients are poor in any case!—but, rather, as human beings no longer anxious, no longer prisoners of anxiety about survival.

The picture Theissen[26] gives of vagabond radicalism reflects primarily the Sayings-source. Here, in brief, is what he says in his essay in *Novum Testamentum* (1977):

In the first century, Palestine suffered increasingly from economic and political crises. The ordinary people found themselves in ever-shifting economic distress (p. 193). "Social uprootedness" took many forms: emigration, new settlements, brigandage, resistance struggles, and vagabond radicalism. By "social uprootedness" Theissen understands the abandonment of an original residence and a break with familiar norms ("deviant behavior," p. 161). From the sociological standpoint, then, vagabond radicalism was a form of social uprootedness consequent upon a crisis in society. The crisis in this case was extensive, and vagabond radicalism was but a "marginal" consequence of it, its representatives being groups on the fringe of a social stratum now threatened by decline, as well as outsiders and, above all, young people (p. 194).

There is little to object to in this sociological classification of vagabond radicalism. Moreover, the picture given in this essay is a decided improvement on the presentation of the movement in an earlier essay in the *Zeitschrift für Theologie und Kirche* (1973). There Theissen had given almost no sociological context; as a result, the wandering preachers appeared as strange outsiders in a society that was otherwise living a "normal" life (see, e.g., p. 262).

We do have objections, however, to Theissen's picture of the "ethos" of the wandering radicals and of their relationship to the majority of the population. He understands the radical "ethos" as the expression of a de facto existence without home, possessions, and family. Matthew 6:25 ("Do not be anxious"), for example, is a reflection of the life of "wandering charismatics who travel about the land propertyless and unemployed."[27] They live in fact as beggars but they look upon themselves as different and avoid the usual forms of begging.[28] Like beggars they make no plans, but "interpret" this behavior as trust in God;[29] they "stylize" their begging, "creatively modify" it.[30] In ZTK (p. 260) Theissen spoke of "beggary of a higher order."

Later, Theissen speaks in NovTest (p. 195) of a "movement of religious renewal" that failed but at least sought new directions. It is not clear, however, in what the positive accomplishment of the group consisted, since Theissen does not concretize these general ideas. What he says about the content of the radical "ethos" has to do exclusively with the wanderers' own interpretations of their vagabond existence, which was incomprehensible to the nonwandering majority of the population.[31] Although in his sociological reflections of 1977 Theissen sees the connection between vagabond radicalism and the situation of the majority of the people, he does not succeed in establishing a relation between the followers of Jesus and the life of the average Jewish citizen. To the nonwandering radicals, the wandering radicals have nothing to say that is connected with their own kind of life; at any rate their preaching to "sympathizers" is not concerned with the radical ethos. This is how Theissen in ZTK (especially p. 260) and in Sociology (pp. 8ff.) must be understood.

In his 1977 essay Theissen is still hindered by the picture he drew in 1973: he does see that the majority of the people lived in economic distress, but he does not see that the wandering radicals saw their kind of existence as part of their message to all of Israel, as shown in Mt. 6:25ff.,Q (the anxiety about "what we shall eat" is the anxiety not only of beggars and wandering radicals but of all "ordinary people"; the exhortations to freedom from care in an attempt to reject hunger as master are meant for all). Sociological and religio-sociological analyses cannot prescind from an effort to come to grips with the content of textual statements; Theissen, however, either concludes too directly from text to situation without considering the intention and social function of the text, or else he uses ambiguous words to describe the intention of the text (e.g., "poverty ethos," "afamilial ethos"; it is not clear what "ethos" means here).[32]

We return now to the missionary discourse. Luke 10:4b,Q (?) says: " . . . and salute no one on the road." The purpose of this instruction is to keep the (magically understood) power of the messenger as bearer of blessing from being diminished by a greeting (see 2 Kings 4:29).

The rule for messengers also says: "Whatever house you enter, first say, 'Peace be to this house!' And if a son of peace is there, your peace shall rest upon him; but if not, it shall return to you. And remain in the same house, eating and drinking what they provide, for the laborer deserves his wages; do not go from house to house" (Mt. 10:11-13,Q→ Lk. 10:5-7; see Mk. 6:10; Lk. 9:4).

The messengers enter a house, evidently without making a deliberate choice of it, and deliver the peace they are carrying; it is to the father of the family that they deliver it. If the peace is accepted, the house serves as a base for the messengers of Jesus. The food they receive is not a kindly gift but a reward that is earned. Compare the practice signaled in 2 Kings 4:8–10; Acts 16:15; and Josephus, *Jewish War* 6, 307. Josephus says of Jeshua, son of Ananias, that "those who gave him food he never thanked"; that is, as a prophet he had a right to maintenance.

It could be, of course, that the son of peace and his family did not have enough to eat for themselves; now, suddenly, one more mouth to feed! It is obvious that given the poverty of ordinary folk in Palestine one more to feed could create a real economic problem (see bTaan 23b). The compulsion to change quarters could therefore have an economic explanation. In any case we need not think of a lengthy stay. The son of peace, the father of the family, who accepted the messenger's peace for his household, was certainly himself a follower of Jesus. He was therefore a potential wandering prophet for whom, as for the other wandering prophet, family ties had to come second to the obligation of service to God and the following of Jesus (Mt. 10:37,Q—see Mk. 8:21,Q—sees the severance from family from the standpoint of an adult male).

Heal the sick in it and say to them, "The kingdom of God has come near to you" [Mt. 10:7, 8a,Q— Lk. 10:9; see Lk. 9:2; Mk. 6:12].

Acceptance by the householder brought peace and the beginning of God's reign to the entire household and therefore probably to the entire village. This meant liberation from anxiety and the visible beginning of salvation in the healing of the sick (see 2 Kings 4:14–17). That acceptance or rejection of the messengers had immediate consequences for the entire town is shown by this next saying.

And wherever they do not receive you, when you leave that town shake off the dust from your feet [Mt. 10:14,Q— Lk. 9:5; 10:10; Mk. 6:11; see Acts 13:51; 18:6; 22:23; Lk. 9:52f.].

The gesture of shaking off the dust is not to be understood as a curse that harms the rejecters. It expresses, rather, the fact that by rejecting God's messengers the town has drawn down God's judgment upon itself, and the messengers have no choice but to leave. The action of the latter rids them of the remnants of their contact with the town, as though otherwise the collective judgment might include them as well if they were still in the town and still had its dust upon them (see Gen. 19:12ff.).

A careful distinction must be made between curse and proclamation of judgment. The messengers do not see themselves as judges who decide whether God's condemnation is to strike the town. They proclaim the judgment but do not use it as an instrument. In any case these followers of Jesus have renounced cursing and judging, as we discuss in section III of this chapter, below.

The missionary discourse ends in a judgment saying that here sums up this important aspect of the practice of the Q prophets: "I tell you, it shall be more tolerable on that day for Sodom than for that town" (Mt. 10:15,Q→ Lk. 10:12).

The story of the rescue of Lot from Sodom (Gen. 19:12ff.; 19:24ff.) is helpful in understanding the Sayings-source as a whole. The Sayings-source makes explicit reference to the destruction of Sodom: Mt. 10:15,Q; Mt. 11:23,Q. Luke 17:28f. ("Likewise as it was in the days of Lot—they ate, they drank, they bought, they sold, they planted, they built, but on the day when Lot went out from Sodom fire and brimstone rained from heaven and destroyed them all") was perhaps subsequently composed (by Luke) by analogy with the Q saying in Mt. 24:37-39,Q. In Q Sodom is the symbol of the terrible destruction of an entire city as the result of God's judgment. The transgression of Sodom, however, is not paralleled with the transgression of the towns of Israel whose destruction the Q prophets announce. The towns of Israel reject the messengers of Jesus or Jesus himself, and this is not a violation of the rights of guests as in Sodom but a rejection of the message of Jesus.[33] As Lot fled the city with his wife and children, so the messengers of Jesus shake off the dust of the towns that are destined for destruction. There can be no more contact with these towns, for otherwise those remaining in contact will be caught up in the destruction—as Lot's wife was when she looked back. "Flee for your life; do not look back or stop anywhere in the valley; flee to the hills, lest you be consumed" (Gen. 19:17). Sodom's destruction by fire and brimstone is the second element in the story that plays a role in the Sayings-source: it will go even worse for the towns of Galilee that reject the message of Jesus. The messengers of Jesus play the part at once of Lot and of the people who announce the disaster.

II. GOD OF THE ORDINARY PEOPLE AND UTOPIAN VISION OF HUMANITY

Anxiety about the minimum for survival turns human beings into its victims, its slaves, so that they are capable of thinking, feeling, and doing only what this anxiety tells them to do. To this anxiety the disciples of Jesus whom we meet in the Sayings-source oppose their own utopian vision: human beings (they say) are more than food and clothing (Mt. 6:25,Q).

We see what human beings really are when we see them in the presence of God. Anxious fear of persecution, spite, and even death has forced to their knees many who confess Jesus. It has taken control of them so that they no longer dare say they are Jesus people. The Jesus people of the Sayings-source offer their own utopian vision to overcome this anxiety. Before God (they say) human beings contain something more than other human beings can kill. They can hold their heads high, for all their hairs are numbered by God. It is God who has the last word about a person; God and not the executioners, is one's master (Mt. 10:28-31,Q).

The image that the Jesus people of Q have of God and, closely connected with this, the utopian vision they have of human beings as they really are—

before God—are of supreme importance for these Jesus people; the image and the vision are their polar star. The purpose of the utopian vision is not to depict a future, other world of God, but to help realize the reign of God as God's absolute claim over human beings in their present life, and thus to help them live a human life that is something "more" than can be destroyed by hunger and death.

The Jesus people did of course share with other groups of early Christians the eschatological expectation of the (proximately) coming Son of man, the divine judgment, and the kingdom of God. We must be clear, however, that in their eyes the reign of God meant first and foremost that God is *Kyrios* ("Lord") and also *Pater* ("Father"). These statements moreover asserted not only God's absolute claim on the followers of Jesus but also God's universal claim on the world, as is clear from Mt. 11:25,Q, where God is called "Father, Lord of heaven and earth."

The concrete situation in which the claim of God and the utopian vision of humanity lead the followers of Jesus to adopt a new outlook is clear. The situation is the need to liberate themselves, by means of real trust in God, from the throttling grip of fear of martyrdom and from anxiety about survival. God as Father and Lord liberates human beings from the other lords who seek to control them. But other situations and temptations are also discernible, which show how this understanding of God sensitizes human beings to structures marked by violence, force, and domination.

A detailed justification for the rejection of other lords is given in connection with the assessment of possessions and wealth in (*a*) Mt. 6:19-21,Q and (*b*) Mt. 6:24,Q: (*a*) "Do not lay up for yourselves treasures on earth, where moth and rust consume and where thieves break in and steal, but lay up for yourselves treasures in heaven, where neither moth nor rust consumes and where thieves do not break in and steal. For where your treasure is, there will your heart be also." (*b*) "No one can serve two masters; for either he will hate the one and love the other, or he will be devoted to the one and despise the other. You cannot serve God and mammon."

Both "mammon," an Aramaic word for possessions and property (in money, real estate, slaves), and the term "treasures" designate wealth. The activity of the rich is pictured as an amassing of treasure and a serving of mammon. Luke 12:16-21, the story of the rich farmer, doubtless provides a valid illustration of this attitude. For in fact the stockpiling of grain and the filling of chests with gold, silver, and fine clothing are some ways in which the rich of this world lay up "treasures" for themselves. According to the messengers of Jesus, one ought not lead that kind of life.

It is unclear, however, what the rich should do if they accept the message in these sayings. There is no reflection here on a concrete alternative behavior for rich people: for example, a renunciation of possessions. Luke therefore provides an interpretation of the saying about treasure. In themselves the two sayings give no concrete exhortation. They simply state a principle, which says that as long as the rich are rich they are on the wrong side. That this is in fact the meaning of these sayings is shown by the first arguments given.

First a pragmatic argument: treasures are endangered things. The proverbial anxiety of the rich is recalled—but with the conclusion being drawn here that they should keep away from riches. This abstention is not to be confused with an interior detachment from riches.

The second argument, which is materially the same in both sayings, is more important: wealth becomes master of the rich as a *kyrios* is master of a slave. The human being becomes dependent, completely dependent, on possessions. The two sayings paint a vivid and unequivocal picture of this dependency. Dependence on possessions is the dependence of an attachment of the heart, comparable to the love and dependence of a slave on a *kyrios*. "Love" and "dependence" should not be interpreted too narrowly as referring to an isolated emotional relationship; rather, emotional and social ties go together. For this reason God and possessions are absolute alternatives; possessions are a kind of god.

The peculiar character of this attitude to wealth becomes clearer if we compare it with the earliest Jesus tradition. There, as here, no appeal is made to the rich; the speaker does not even envisage such an appeal. In the earliest Jesus tradition, however, the hope is for an eschatological reversal, a balancing out of lots; the element in the life of the rich that attracts attention is their enjoyment of life's good things. Here in the Sayings-source, on the other hand, attention is focused on the control that possessions exercise over human beings. Correspondingly, the emphasis is not on the eschatological result but on the distance between the rich and God.

These differences between the earliest Jesus tradition and the Sayings-source in their attitude to wealth have theological consequences. For, even though the living conditions of both groups of disciples are on the whole comparable, in the earliest Jesus tradition the rule of God finds expression directly in a graphic reversal of social destinies, whereas the Jesus people of the Sayings-source always think consistently in terms of lordship: either God is Lord or mammon is lord. Thus the messengers of Jesus think through the situation of the rich with greater theological consistency.

We should not block our own access to this kind of thinking by saying, for example, "But the rich too must be accepted as children of God." If the rich had accepted the logic of these sayings and drawn the proper conclusions, they would have ceased to be rich. In other words, one could conclude from these sayings that one ought to renounce possessions. We must understand, however, that in fact no appeal along these lines is being made to the rich. (Note that there is no non-Christian analogy for the penetrating insight shown in these sayings, despite, for example, many parallel metaphorical uses of *thesauros,* "treasure.") Insofar as these sayings of the Sayings-source differ from what is said in the earliest Jesus tradition, they are the result of experience in following Jesus. The rich of Palestine were not among the disciples of Jesus; the profound insight expressed in these sayings explains why they were not.

The story of the temptation of Jesus (Mt. 4:1–11,Q) must likewise be interpreted in light of the image of God that the Sayings-source manifests. The reason is that in all three temptations Jesus gives the devil answers that refer to

God's claim to be sole Lord. The situation of the followers of Jesus is existentially central here, as it is in the assessment of riches.

> The devil said to him: "If you are the Son of God, command that these stones turn into bread." But he answered: "It is written: 'Not on bread alone does man live.' " The devil took him into the holy city and set him on the pinnacle of the temple and said to him: "If you are the Son of God, throw yourself down; for it is written: 'He has given his angels orders about you, and they will carry you in their hands, lest you stub your foot against a stone' (Ps. 91:11f.)." Jesus said to him: "It is written: 'You shall not tempt the Lord your God' (Deut. 6:16)." And the devil took him up to a very high mountain and said to him: "All this will I give you if you pay me homage." And Jesus answered him: "It is written: 'The Lord your God shall you adore and him alone shall you serve' (Deut. 6:13)." Then the devil departed from him.[34]

It is important from the standpoint of method not to isolate the story of the temptations but to interpret it in the context of Q, for otherwise it becomes ambiguous. Furthermore, parallel motifs from the history of religions should not influence the interpretation unless they are recognizable in the text itself. For example, one may not say that the first temptation refers to a Jewish expectation that the Messiah will repeat the miracle of the manna in the wilderness.[35] The desire that stones be turned into bread is not a reference to the miracle of the manna, since the manna was bread that fell from heaven.

Nor should the figure of the devil be made the focal point of the temptations. Jesus rejects the temptations, not because it is the devil who suggests them but because he will have nothing to do with what is suggested. Universal rule, for example, is rejected because the will to rule the world violates God's claim to be sole ruler, and not simply because the devil wants to be adored in exchange for world rule. In other words, the content of the temptations is serious challenges made to the followers of Jesus, who identify themselves with him. In this story he represents his followers, and the temptations are demands that have been made of the Jesus people, and which they put in the mouth of the devil because they wish to make clear the attack on God these demands represent.[36]

The first temptation, which is to turn stones into bread, is connected with the exhortation against anxiety about survival (Mt. 6:25ff.,Q). The messengers of Jesus and the sons of peace trust in God and live from hand to mouth. How often must others not have said to them: "If Jesus is God's Son and if God is Lord of the world, why does he not put an end to your hunger (and perhaps everyone's hunger) with a miracle?" The answer is in substance the same as in Mt. 6:25,Q: "Then bread would be our master."

God could, of course, will to turn all the stones on earth into bread. The issue here is not whether or not Jesus and his followers are to rely on miracles. The issue is which miracles are to be rejected because of what they imply. If the disciples wanted miraculous bread of this kind and perhaps wanted even to produce it themselves, they would be focusing on bread and not on God and would thereby be subjecting themselves to a false lord. It is easy to imagine such wishes being expressed in the starving Palestine of the time. The temptation to imagine miraculous future solutions may in fact have attacked the very followers of Jesus. The greater their distress, after all, the more ready people are to embrace illusions. "Illusions," because *this kind* of expectation of miracles is an illusion even for followers of Jesus (although his followers do not reject miracles in principle). They reject this kind of reliance on miracles, however, not because it is illusory but because they see it as a flouting of God's claim upon human beings. They understand the illusory character of the miracle at a much deeper level: as a radical attack by anxiety about survival. It is this anxiety that guides the wish and reduces its victims to submission by means of the illusion.

The story of the temptations is not concerned with the temptations of *Jesus,* seen as someone apart. It would therefore be incorrect to think that the devil tempts Jesus to a miraculous production of bread because Jesus is now hungry owing to his stay in the wilderness. We must always take into account those who are telling the story as their own. The people here telling of Jesus' hunger in the wilderness are people who live with hunger every day. They make no artificial distinction, either historical or theological, between themselves and Jesus. His rejection of the temptation means that they too reject the temptation that hunger causes them.

The second temptation has to do with trust in God in the face of the death of which Mt. 10:28-31,Q speaks. You say you trust God so utterly that you accept your possible death as God's will? You live as though nothing could happen to you? Well, then, let us see how great your trust in God really is! A leap from the pinnacle of the temple will force God to send angels, lest you end up smashed against the pavement. The aim of the temptation is to pervert trust in God into an illusory attempt to make God and the angels dance to a human tune. Jesus might also have answered: human beings are more than their deaths, but if I jump from the temple in order to compel God to rescue me, I am attempting to control God and am thereby at the same time myself controlled by fear of death. For it is fear of death that dictates such desires.

The need to resist a desire for miracles made attractive by distress was not an idle invention of the Sayings-source. This is clear from the terrible story told by Josephus in the *Jewish War* (6, 285f.). A few hours before the temple area was stormed by the Romans, 6,000 people had taken refuge in a building that was still standing although everything around was in flames. A prophet had told them that they should wait there for a sign of deliverance. They all perished. Such a prophet could not have come from the messengers of the Sayings-source. In their eyes to behave in this way would have been to tempt God, because it turned human beings into passive victims.

The third temptation tells of illusory desires, the significance of which in the Palestine of that day is still well known to us. Many people were hoping to be delivered from Roman domination and to see Israel ruling the world. Israel's weakness and the widespread disastrous political and economic condition of Palestine before the war led to the cultivation of fantastic hopes.

Prophecy and the hopes based on it played a major part in the political and military conflict, particularly in the form of directly political prophecy and political hopes. Especially important in this context was the following oracle:

Their [the Jews'] chief inducement to go to war was an equivocal oracle also found in their sacred writings, announcing that at that time a man from their country would become monarch of the whole world. This they took to mean the triumph of their own race, and many of their scholars were wildly out in their interpretation. In fact the oracle pointed to the accession of Vespasian; for it was in Judea that he was proclaimed emperor.[37]

In the conflict the political adversaries also confronted each other as prophets who were in disagreement. The people understood the prophecy in question as announcing that the Jews would rule the world; Josephus, spokesman for the pro-Roman party, interpreted it in a pro-Roman way: it referred to the world-wide rule of Vespasian, the Roman emperor.

On the Roman side, world rule was not simply a wish, it was asserted as a reality; the Romans saw themselves as masters of the world. On the other side, rebellious groups in Palestine dreamed of world rule; they wanted to be the masters at last. In the story of the temptations this desire to rule the world is rejected as an attack on God. Given the part played by world rule in the political ideology of the Roman empire, we may not eliminate the anti-Roman element in the third temptation. The temptation addresses both the hopes of the Zealots and others for rule and the ideology of the Romans. The desire for domination is anti-God. Here again the dialectical insight that is present in the first two temptations, when seen in the context of Mt. 6:25ff.,Q and Mt. 10:28ff.,Q, must be taken into account: Those who cultivate such desires and notions are attempting to usurp God's rule; they are at once greedy for power and victims of their own weakness. The focus on God as sole Lord is profoundly "anarchic." The Jesus people of Q did not want to be rulers and did not want to let themselves be overcome by desires for power (desires which would be utterly illusory in their case). God's lordship excludes every other lordship.

The point of the temptation story is not to criticize a Christology of Jesus as wonder-worker, in which miracles prove the legitimacy of the person of God. The desire for miracles that is criticized here is criticized because of its content. The fault lies not in expecting miracles from Jesus or his followers; it is in the kind of miracles that are desired. The poor of the Q movement had made their own the hope that the blind would gain sight, the lame walk, and so on. These were hopes that did not make human beings victims of their wretched-ness, but were based on concrete experiences. On the other hand, the hope that stones would turn into bread was a hope that deceives the hopers and renders them helpless. The belief that God's rule had begun in the healings worked by Jesus made these people strong and put them in command of their lives. The results in the lives of those concerned force us, therefore, to distinguish between an illusory hope of miracles and a serious hope of miracles.

The idea of God that the Q people have is extremely authoritarian. It is not possible to express God's lordship in a more radical way. True enough, "fatherhood" conveys a sense of security (the hairs of our heads are numbered; God's all-embracing providential care), but it does so without introducing any weakness into the authoritarian, patriarchal picture of God: It is God who determines the lives of human beings. On the other hand, the authoritarian God of the ordinary people is not to be confused with the authoritarian God of the upper classes who make use of the strong God in order to assert their own interests against those of others. The authoritarian God of the ordinary people is not a tool to be used against others who do not want what they want; rather, this God strengthens the faithful against the violent storms to which their life exposes them. Anxiety about survival and the fear of martyrdom seek to grip them; they are menaced by dreams in which they triumph over all these things and perhaps even turn the tables so as to say, "Now we're the masters!"

The authoritarian God of the lowly makes them certain that they are human beings, even though one might think of them as permanently downtrodden. God also makes them strong enough to take command of their own lives, even though they are incapable of transforming these lives in a spectacular way.

The discussion of the content of the miracles and expectations expressed in the temptation story brings to light the central importance of the idea of God, for it is this that gives direction in case of conflict. In general, the idea of God also determines the special way in which the Q people deal with those who reject their message and Jesus as well. This will be the subject of the next section.

III. PROCLAMATION OF JUDGMENT AND LOVE OF ENEMIES

1. The Problem

From the earlier Jesus tradition (Lk. 6:10f.,Q; Mt. 11:2-5,Q) the followers of Jesus who express themselves in the Sayings-source took over the idea that Jesus had brought the good news to the poor, and they applied this to themselves. The poor whom Jesus declared blessed are now the persecuted messengers of Jesus. The message of the dawning of God's reign in the good news preached to the poor and in the miracles done for the lame and the blind becomes for the Q people the decisive point that leads to a parting of ways: "And blessed is he who takes no offense at me" (Mt. 11:6,Q).

The followers of Jesus in the Sayings-source are poor like most Jews, although not all are destitute (ptōchoi). "Good news for the poor," however, no longer means for them the hope that the reign of God will bring compensation for the misery of the poor. For them it means deliverance from lords—hunger especially—that seek to make human beings subject to them. The problem of wealth is seen in terms of an alternative—the service of mammon—to the reign of God. Yet the gulf between rich and poor is not mentioned. The conflict that concerns these people and elicits a permanent commitment from them is the conflict that the message of Jesus has created within the Jewish people. The actualizations already mentioned of the earlier Jesus tradition by Q (Mt. 5:11f.,Q; 11:6,Q) relate to this conflict. We shall have to inquire later on how the conflict relates to social divisions. In the Sayings-source it is not presented as a social conflict.

Experiences of this conflict are reflected in almost all the texts of the Sayings-source. Thus it provides the backdrop for the extensive complex of Q sayings about judgment, which, at least at first hearing, inevitably seem repulsive to today's reader because of their gloomy and unyielding rigor. Destruction by God's judgment is announced for Jerusalem and other towns of the country. For example: " . . . it shall be more tolerable on the day of judgment for the land of Sodom and Gomorrah than for that town" (Mt. 10:15,Q). Gloomy prophecies—and prophecies that were fulfilled, for the country suffered cruelly in the Jewish war.

Gloomy sayings about judgment stand alongside radiant promises: "But blessed are the eyes which see what you see [and the ears which hear what you hear]" (Mt. 13:16f.,Q). They see the miracles worked in the lame and the blind, they hear the good news for the poor and see therein the beginning of God's reign. But then again come sayings that reflect a fearful reality, sayings that prophesy judgment because of the rejection of the message about Jesus.

How did the messengers of Jesus come to combine the two? We would completely misunderstand the movement if we saw it as a group of the "quiet folk of the country" who would say, for example, "The few who accept the message—and we are those few—will be saved; the many who do not belong to our pious little circle will be destroyed." In fact, as far as we know, there is no (religio-)sociological analogy for the movement we witness here. This little minority does not understand itself as a self-contained enclave of salvation, an eschatological remnant. In this respect it is in crucial continuity with the earliest Jesus tradition. Its message and activity are wholly directed in a positive way to the many who reject the message of Jesus. These people run after their enemies, and the running after is to be taken quite literally in the case of the wandering prophets. They practice love of enemies and proclaim judgment; in fact, they practice love by means of their proclamation of judgment.

We shall advance step by step in an effort to understand this paradox: the texts of the Sayings-source allow us to reconstruct the negative experience that the messengers of Jesus had of rejection, hostility, and persecution; against the background of this concrete experience, the call for love of enemies in Q can be understood as a call for a concrete behavior; the sayings about judgment are part of this behavior. Love of enemies is not a behavior reserved for special moments of life, but the common denominator, the clamp as it were, that holds together the entire behavior and the message of the followers of Jesus.

2. The Experience of Hostility

The messengers of Jesus are persecuted (*diōkein* Mt. 23:34–36,Q; probably Mt. 5:44f.,Q); they are reviled (*oneidizein,* Mt. 5:11f.,Q); they are brought to the synagogues for questioning (Mt. 10:19f.,Q);[38] stonings and killings occur

(Mt. 23:37-39,Q; *apokteinein*, also in Mt. 23: 34-36, Q, and probably in Mt. 23: 29-31, Q). The messengers experience their persecutors as enemies (Mt. 5:44f.,Q) and see themselves threatened like sheep among wolves (Mt. 10:16,Q); they say that even in the eyes of God these enemies are wicked men (*poneroi*, Mt. 5:44f.,Q; Mt. 7:7-11,Q). The expression "this [wicked] generation" (*hē genea tautē*, Mt. 11:16,Q; 12:39,Q; 12:41f.,Q) echoes all these experiences.

The rejection that the messengers have experienced is expressed pictorially in the parable of the playing children who reject all offers. "But to what shall I compare this generation? It is like children[39] sitting in the streets and calling to those who come,/'We piped to you, and you did not dance;/ we wailed, and you did not mourn' " (Mt. 11:16f.,Q). How often had not salvation been offered to them! "And you would not!" (Mt. 23:37-39,Q).

The rejection, persecution, and killing of Jesus and the rejection, persecution, and killing of his messengers are not contrasted but, rather, mentioned in one and the same breath. It is almost self-evident that the death of Jesus is included when mention is made of the killing of the prophets. In the Sayings-source the death of Jesus has a central role in the relation of God to Israel—but this death is not given a soteriological interpretation. "The destiny of Jesus was, rather, that of all messengers of wisdom."[40] It is the persecution and killing of Jesus *and* of his followers that brings judgment on Israel.

We are not told what concrete form the reviling of Jesus' messengers took, but we do know the insults with which Jesus was rejected: "For John came neither eating nor drinking, and they say, 'He has a demon'; the Son of man came eating and drinking, and they say, 'Behold, a glutton and a drunkard, a friend of tax collectors and sinners!' Yet wisdom is justified by her children" (Mt. 11:18f.,Q).

The way in which John the Baptist was treated was already unjust; his asceticism was attributed to demons and used as a pretext for not listening to him. The objection to Jesus, on the other hand, is that he is not an ascetic. For the Sayings-source, then, the objection that "he is a glutton and a drunkard, a friend of tax collectors and sinners" is likewise unjustified.[41] It is a pretext for rejecting him. He will be vindicated against this reproach by the children of wisdom.

The missionary discourse describes a concrete situation in which the followers of Jesus are rejected. They are not received in a town, and they leave it in haste, for it has drawn down judgment upon itself (Mt. 10:14,Q; see above). Nonetheless they continue to pursue Israel and to have the same sad experience: "How often would I have gathered your children together as a hen (gathers) her brood under her wings, and you would not!" (Mt. 23:37-39,Q). The messengers of Jesus must be prepared to accept the cross (Mt. 10:38,Q)—and, in the light of all we know about their lot, the word "cross" was not meant metaphorically.[42] For it was not out of the question for the political leaders of Israel to have embarrassing persons of Israel flogged or even handed over to the Romans for execution by crucifixion.[43]

The experience of rejection is also reflected in Mt. 24:37-39,Q. As in the days of Noah before the flood, people live, unsuspecting and indifferent, eating and drinking, marrying and giving in marriage: we can see the messengers of Jesus there, trying with all their powers of persuasion to awaken these people. "But you would not!"

3. Love of Enemies

The messengers of Jesus describe themselves as defenseless and threatened, like sheep among wolves, and as consciously following the path of renunciation of force (Mt. 5:39f.,Q). The defenselessness and the renunciation of force have one and the same source: they are dictated by the positive goal of the messengers of Jesus in dealing with all of Israel, even the Israel whose rejection the messengers constantly experience. Apart from their connection with the commandment of love of enemies and their location in the Sayings-source as a whole, the defenselessness and renunciation of force would be ambiguous. Such an attitude might, for example, be a kind of masochism bent on martyrdom and serve as a means of augmenting the enemy's guilt. Or the show of nonviolence might be intended as a political demonstration, a statement against those who follow the way of violence in fighting for their freedom.

In fact, some scholars—Poul Hoffman and Martin Hengel, in particular—have interpreted the nonviolence of the Q prophets as a political demonstration. The situation as they see it is that the Q prophets oppose Jewish resistance movements and side with the "peace party." The peace party, of whose existence we learn from Josephus, pleads for peace with Rome and for the abandonment of resistance to Rome.

But a political interpretation of the nonviolence and love of enemies promoted in the Sayings-source does not fit the facts there. The enemy in the Sayings-source is not the Romans but those within the Jewish people who reject the prophets. The political conflict between the Jewish people and Rome plays no direct role in the Sayings-source, though it perhaps plays an indirect role in the prophetic provision of Israel's terrible future. In addition, the peace party of Josephus hardly represented the kind of society the Q prophets were seeking. In fact, in political interpretations of Q, the character of the peace party is misrepresented. It was not made up of level-headed, peace-loving individuals but of representatives of the Jewish upper class who, like Josephus himself, were driven by transparently economic interests to seek peace with Rome and who in addition took arms against their own Jewish brethren when they saw their interests threatened by the constant turmoil."

The renunciation of force and the love of enemies preached in the Sayings-source are not intended polemically and as a way of distinguishing a political group. Love of enemies flows, rather, from the positive goal that these people seek. Their desire is that salvation should come even to those who have already rejected it and are hostile to the saving message being preached to them by the Jesus people. God wants to bestow his good gifts even on the wicked, provided they finally agree to listen: "Ask, and it will be given to you; seek, and you will find. . . . Everyone who asks, receives. . . . Or is there someone among you whose son asks him for bread—will he give him a stone? Or if he asks him for a fish, will he give him a snake? Well, then, if you who are wicked know how to give good [good gifts] to your children, how much more will the Father give good things from heaven to those who ask him?" (Mt. 7:7-11,Q; from Harnack's translation).

The addressees here are the enemies of the message of Jesus. They are the wicked who must learn to ask God. They are identical with the wicked of whom it is said in the commandment of love of enemies that God makes the sun to rise even on them (Mt. 5:44f.,Q).[45] In the context of Q the "wicked" are very concrete persons; they are the same as the "enemies" of Mt. 5:44f.,Q. Matthew 7:7-11,Q is therefore not speaking, as is often supposed, of the wickedness of all human beings, nor in very general terms of the certainty all who pray may have of being heard (another widespread interpretation).[46]

Provided you ask, God will give good things to you who are wicked and who constantly reject the message of Jesus. Here again it is clear what an important role the idea of God plays in determining the content preached by the messengers of Jesus. They see God as Father and Creator (Mt. 7:7-11,Q; Mt. 5:44f.) and understand this to imply that salvation and true humanness are available to all human beings, even when it becomes impossible to imagine the enemies of Jesus being converted. God does not give up: "He makes his sun rise on the evil and on the good [and sends rain on the just and on the unjust]" (Mt. 5:44f.,Q).

The messengers of Jesus understand themselves as imitating this God in their action: they intend to bestow love, prayer, and blessing on those who are hostile to them and persecute them.[47] Prayer and blessing are not to be understood as purely verbal actions, any more than love is. In the Sayings-source and in the ancient mind generally, prayer and blessing establish or restore relations of community, just as a curse puts an end to such relations. We must try to get clear in our own minds the spatial imagination at work in these concepts: prayer and blessing create a circle of communion around the one praying and those for whom one prays or blesses. A curse, on the other hand, chases a person away, expels the person from the community, and hands the person over to possible death.[48]

This self-understanding of the messengers of Jesus is without sociological or religio-sociological parallel, as far as we know. In all likelihood, they saw themselves as a cohesive group, though nothing is explicitly said on this point. We can only imagine the organizational form this cohesion took, since we have no information on the subject. It is clear that the group experienced internal difficulties; for example, there were followers of Jesus who confessed him only with their lips (Mt. 7:21-24,Q) and failed to put his instruction into practice.

At the same time, however, the group of Jesus' followers does not define its identity by opposition to outsiders. The reason for this lack of dissociation and the refusal to distinguish between insiders and outsiders becomes clear when we consider these attitudes in the context of the commandment on love of enemies: "If you love those who love you, what reward have you? Do not even the tax collectors do the same? And if you salute only your brethren, what more are you doing than others? Do not even the Gentiles do the same?" (Mt. 5:46-47).

Love your enemies. This means that the group of Jesus' followers is fully conscious of its (sociological) uniqueness. It knows that it is behaving in an unusual way when it takes a positive attitude toward people who not only do not belong to the group (clan, nation, etc.) but are even hostile to the idea of following Jesus. Love of enemies breaks out of the customary forms of solidarity, which is usually seen as extending to a group (however defined) but not to the group's enemies. Love of enemies thus gives expression to a positive intention that includes all human beings or, in this context, all Israel.

The fact that non-Israelites here remain secondary figures even when they become followers of Jesus (Gentile Christians) is not an argument against the comprehensive and universal salvific intention of the Sayings-source. As far as the Q prophets are concerned, people outside Israel are far distant. The prophets have indeed heard of Gentile Christians. They find that the existence of Gentile Christianity renders Israel's sinfulness in God's eyes even more clearly visible (e.g., Mt. 8:10,Q).[49] Even Gentiles in the biblical story become witnesses in the indictment of Israel; for example, the queen of the south and the Ninevites (Mt. 12:41f.,Q): in their day they heeded Solomon and Jonah. The Sayings-source is concerned with Israel, all of Israel and not just good Israelites. It is not legitimate to fault these Jews who are struggling for the salvation of Israel because they have what is in a sense a limited horizon; compared to them Paul was a worldy-wise cosmopolite, for he was in fact a citizen of the Roman empire. It is of theological importance to see that the goal of the Q prophets is comprehensive and universal (in terms of their horizon).

In the Christianity of our own time, love of enemies has often been defined as a removal of all barriers from love of neighbor; as a universal love of humankind that in principle embraces every human being. But such a version of love of enemies is at least open to misunderstanding, since it says "In principle I can love everyone, even an enemy, if I encounter one." For the Q prophets, on the other hand, enemies are concrete individuals in concrete situations. Moreover, the universality of love of enemies does not broaden its task to include all the other possible situations in which love is commanded. The point is not to love everyone in principle but to love persecutors. The universality attaching to love of enemies is a universality derived from the goal: salvation for all Israel (salvation for all). It is this universality of the goal that inevitably requires such persistent efforts toward those who reject this universal salvation.

For the Q prophets, the effort expended in behalf of enemies and the attempt to establish communion with them are not love in the sense of a feeling (as love of enemies has repeatedly been misunderstood to be, especially since the nineteenth century); they are work (Mt. 9:37f.,Q; see above), praxis, the concrete doing of concrete tasks. This means, first and foremost, the constant repetition of the message of Jesus to the very people who are unwilling to hear it, and the constant proclamation of judgment to them.

In our experience Martin Luther King's work and his discourses on love of enemies have facilitated understanding of the Sayings-source. In particular, the initially alienating talk of judgment in the Sayings-source becomes more intelligible in the context of the call to love our enemies, when we see how King regards a direct approach to enemies as necessary and what form the talk of judgment takes in his sermons. King's discourses belong to the history of the influence of the Sayings-source. At the same time, they help the present-day reader of the Bible to understand the Sayings-source. The following passage may help to clarify these points further:

> My friends, we have followed the so-called practical way for too long a time now, and it has led inexorably to deeper confusion and chaos. Time is cluttered with the wreckage of communities which surrendered to hatred and violence. For the salvation of our nation and the salvation of mankind, we must follow another way. This does not mean that we abandon our righteous efforts. With every ounce of our energy we must continue to rid this nation of the incubus of segregation. But we shall not in the process relinquish our privilege and our obligation to love. While abhorring segregation, we shall love the segregationist. This is the only way to create the beloved community.
>
> To our most bitter opponents we say: "We shall match your capacity to inflict suffering by our capacity to endure suffering. We shall meet your physical force with soul force. Do to us what you will, and we shall continue to love you. We cannot in all good conscience obey your unjust laws, because noncooperation with evil is just as much a moral obligation as is cooperation with good. Throw us in jail, and we shall still love you. Bomb our homes and threaten our children, and we shall still love you. Send your hooded perpetrators of violence into our community at the midnight hour and beat us and leave us half dead, and we shall still love you. But be ye assured that we will wear you down by our capacity to suffer. One day we shall win freedom, but not only for ourselves. We shall so appeal to your heart and conscience that we shall win *you* in the process, and our victory will be a double victory.
>
> Love is the more durable power in the world. This creative force, so beautifully exemplified in the life of our Christ, is the most potent instrument available in mankind's quest for peace and security.[50]

4. The Preaching of Judgment

The preaching of judgment occupies considerable space in the texts of the Sayings-source. We noted earlier that the proclamation of judgment is not to be mistaken for a curse but must, rather, be understood as dictated by the positive goal of salvation for all Israel. Its aim is not to deliver the addressees to their unhappy destiny, much less to call down divine punishment.

To the towns of Israel that refuse to listen, the Q prophets announce a terrible destruction. At the same time, however, they travel about precisely in order to keep this disaster from coming upon these enemies. In fact, they call for *metanoia* ("conversion") but, surprisingly, do not do it in so many words. Their hearers have refused to be converted in response to the message of Jesus:

"Woe to you, Chorazin! woe to you, Bethsaida! for if the mighty works done in you had been done in Tyre and Sidon, they would have repented long ago in sackcloth and ashes" (Mt. 11:21,Q; on the refusal of conversion, see Mt. 12:41,Q). Chorazin, Bethsaida, Capernaum—little towns in Galilee—drew down God's judgment on themselves when they rejected Jesus and his messengers. So too did Jerusalem (Mt. 23:37-39,Q), whose destruction is expected: "Behold, your house [= city] is forsaken." Here the destruction of Jerusalem is foreseen prophetically; it is awaited as the final judgment of God. For this reason Mt. 23:37-39,Q should under no circumstances be interpreted as a *vaticinium ex eventu* (a prophecy after the fact), a backdated prediction of an event that has already occurred in the time of the speaker.

The severity of this proclamation of judgment by Jews on other Jews in the period before the Jewish war becomes especially clear in the Q sayings on the killing of the prophets.

> Therefore also the Wisdom of God said, "I send you prophets and wise men and scribes, some of whom you will kill and persecute," that upon you may come all the blood shed on earth, from the blood of Abel to the blood of Zechariah, whom you murdered between the temple and the altar. Amen, I tell you, all this will come upon this generation [Mt. 23:34-36,Q].

> Woe to you! for you build the tombs of the prophets and say, "If we had lived in the days of our fathers, we would not have been guilty of the blood of the prophets." Thus you witness against yourselves, that you are the sons of those who murdered the prophets [Mt. 23:29-31,Q].

This generation of prophet killers is coming to an end. The messengers repeatedly call for a decision; such a call is in fact implicit in each of these judgment sayings. But explicit calls for a decision are also found; for example, Mt. 11:6,Q, "Blessed is he who takes no offense at me" (see also, e.g., Mt. 10:32f.,Q). The message of Jesus is a sword that divides families (Mt. 10:34f.,Q) and inaugurates the great division: "Do you think that I have come to bring peace on earth? I have not come to bring peace, but a sword. I have come to set a man against his father, and a daughter against her mother, and a wife against her mother-in-law; [and a man's foes will be those of his own household]."

This saying makes it clear once more that the message of Jesus with its call for decision led to very real divisions. The statement that families will be torn apart is to be taken literally in its context in Q. In Mt. 10:34f.,Q a saying of Jesus explains why people abandon their families in the name of Jesus, and it provides justification for the abandonment. If a family does not unanimously decide to accept the message of Jesus, then the followers of Jesus must withdraw from it. They must "shake the dust from their feet" like the messengers in Mt. 10:14,Q (see above), because otherwise the destruction wrought by God's judgment will come upon them as well.

The fact that families are thus rent is understood as a sign of the last times. And indeed the fear that the confusion preceding the end would destroy families was widespread at this time; see, for example, Mk. 13:12 (though here the destruction is an apocalyptic prediction; Mt. 10:34f.,Q, on the other hand, is not a prediction). In fact, the terrifying vision is already a reality. Matthew 10:35,Q makes explicit reference by its formulation to Mic. 7:6 and thus shows that in the rending of families at the present time an Old Testament prophecy of apocalyptic distress is now fulfilled.

The messengers of Jesus flee when they see that a town is now under judgment; they flee a family that refuses to listen to the message of Jesus. At the same time, however, they pursue those who refuse to listen. They express this paradox in a vivid picture: "What do you think? If a man has a hundred sheep, and one of them has gone astray, does he not leave the ninety-nine [in the pasture] and go in search of the one that went astray? And if he finds it, truly, I say to you, he rejoices over it more than over the ninety-nine that never went astray" (Mt. 18:12f.,Q). In the context of the Sayings-source this parable has a concrete meaning. It describes pictorially the situation of Jesus (as seen by the Q prophets) and the situation of the prophets themselves: They pursue the strayed sheep, they pursue Israel, which refuses to listen, and the Jews who reject the message of Jesus.[51] They are repeatedly forced to proclaim judgment, but they continue to pursue and to hope for the joy of finding the lost.

The situation of the Q prophets as depicted here will doubtless strike us as extraordinary, and this not only by comparison with our own utterly different situation today. For after the interpretation given of them the question inevitably arises: Can such people have ever existed? The question requires a historical answer, and we have one at hand in the form of a fully reliable report by Josephus about a prophet in Jerusalem.

An incident more alarming still had occurred four years before the war at a time of exceptional peace and prosperity for the City. One Jeshua son of Ananias, a very ordinary yokel, came to the feast at which every Jew is expected to set up a tabernacle for God. As he stood in the Temple he suddenly began to shout: "A voice from the east, a voice from the west, a voice from the four winds, a voice against Jerusalem and the Sanctuary, a voice against bridegrooms and brides, a voice against the whole people." Day and night he uttered this cry as he went through all the streets. Some of the more prominent citizens, very annoyed at these ominous words, laid hold of the fellow and beat him savagely. Without saying a word in his own defence or for the private information of his persecutors, he persisted in shouting the same warning as before.

The Jewish authorities, rightly concluding that some supernatural force was responsible for the man's behaviour, took him before the Roman procurator. There, though scourged till his flesh hung in ribbons, he neither begged for mercy nor shed a tear, but lowering his voice to the most mournful of tones answered every blow with "Woe to Jerusalem!" When Albinus—for that was the procurator's name—demanded to know who he was, where he came from and why he uttered such cries, he made no reply whatever to the questions but endlessly repeated his lament over the City, till Albinus decided he was a madman and released him.

All the time till the war broke out he never approached another citizen or was seen in conversation, but daily as if he has learnt a prayer by heart he recited his lament: "Woe to Jerusalem!" Those who daily cursed him he never cursed; those who gave him food he never thanked; his only response to anyone was that dismal foreboding. His voice was heard most of all at the feasts. For seven years and five months he went on ceaselessly, his voice as strong as ever and his vigour unabated, till during the siege after seeing the fulfilment of his foreboding he was silenced. He was going round on the wall uttering his piercing cry: "Woe again to the City, the people, and the Sanctuary!" and as he added a last word: "Woe to me also!" a stone shot from an engine struck him, killing him instantly. Thus he uttered those same forebodings to the very end.[52]

The many similarities between this prophet of judgment and the Q prophets need not be spelled out in detail. Critical for an understanding of Jeshua is the question whether in fact he had nothing to say but "that dismal foreboding." Because of Josephus' purpose in telling the story of this prophet he is interested in him as a prophet of disaster. He is using Jeshua as evidence that through sheer foolishness the Jews wrongly interpreted the signs and prophecies of disaster for Israel and thus made themselves (and not the Romans) responsible for their own destruction. But because of Josephus' tendentiousness, though not because of that alone, we may doubt that this prophet is correctly to be understood as a prophet of judgment who had no positive message of any kind.

The man responds to torture and blows with his saying about doom, not with a curse or a plea. He does not justify or defend himself. Like the Q prophets he refuses to stop repeating his message. Like the Q prophets he addresses himself to the entire population of Israel. Despite the negative report, therefore, his behavior makes it very likely that his goal was a positive one. The fact that the man did not justify or defend himself and that he did not curse is a puzzle to Josephus. He therefore regards Jeshua as someone possessed and as an instrument of God with no will of his own.

We may well think, then, that despite Josephus' negative description of him, Jeshua son of Ananias closely resembled the Q prophets in his message, his behavior, his destiny, and his social background. The social location of the Q prophets that has thus far been attempted is given additional support by this passage in Josephus. The Q prophets, like Jeshua, were far removed from the powerful and prosperous in Israel and were considered dangerous to that group; they were therefore persecuted (with Roman help, to some extent). The gulf between the followers of Jesus and those who rejected them was in part a social gulf. But of course the Q prophets were also rejected by people of their own class, as the division within families attests.

3

The Following of Christ as Solidarity between Rich, Respected Christians and Poor, Despised Christians (Gospel of Luke)

I. THE APPROACH TO LUKE'S SOCIAL MESSAGE

To a much greater extent than the Gospels of Matthew and Mark, the Gospel of Luke transmits traditional material in which the problem created by the social distinction of poor and rich plays a part. We need think only of the Beatitude of the poor and the parallel woe-saying on the rich (Lk. 6:20-26), the story of the rich but foolish farmer (12:16-21), the story of the rich man and poor Lazarus (16:19-31), and the exemplary conduct of Zacchaeus, the rich chief tax collector (19:1-10). If we did not have Luke, we would probably have lost an important, if not the most important, part of the earliest Christian tradition and its intense preoccupation with the figure and message of Jesus as hope of the poor.

Moreover, a continuation of this tradition in the earliest history of the church, down to and including the ascetic worldview of the monks, would hardly have been conceivable without Luke. The third Gospel's sometimes uncompromising statements on social questions subsequently won for its author the reputation of being "very much a socialist thinker."[1] Even those who shy away from this more political classification of Luke's intentions or who regard it as problematic, nonetheless continue to speak of him as "the evangelist of the poor."[2]

Among the interpreters, both practical and scholarly, of this book there have never been lacking those who have refused to take literally its tradition on poverty (especially its sharp criticism of the rich) or who have explained this as a response to a problem of an age now long past.[3] But is it not objectively possible to interpret differently the existence in Luke of an extensive tradition on poverty? Precisely when we take a sociohistorical view of the pre-Lucan stage of these traditions, the evangelist's way of dealing with them can look like an attempt to moderate the originally radical character of the texts.[4] Is Luke, then, really a "pastor to the wealthy"? Once the question is raised we shall find it suspicious that, precisely in Luke, Jesus and especially the apostles and the preachers we meet in Acts frequent the homes of rich and important individuals. Wealthy women in particular play an important role in the circle around Jesus and the apostles (see, e.g., Lk. 8:3 and Acts 16:14).

Finally, Luke's extensive transmission of the texts in question may also be explained in terms of the "accuracy" of an author who not only intends to be faithful to his source material but has ambitiously set out to investigate, from the beginning, everything that has happened. "I in my turn, after carefully (akribōs) going over the whole story from the beginning, have decided to write an ordered account for you, Theophilus, so that your Excellency may learn how well founded the teaching is that you have received" (Lk. 1:3f., JB).

Since our concern in this chapter is to determine Luke's *own* position on social problems, we cannot allow our vision to be distorted by the mere fact that we find in him an extensive tradition of texts on these problems. The fact is in itself susceptible of several and even contradictory interpretations. Even the program set down by Luke the "writer" in the prologue just cited is too general and formal to allow any far-reaching conclusions regarding the theological message of this Gospel. Of course, it would be no less a mistake to isolate individual important texts of Luke and query them for answers to the questions that interest us here. For the real question is precisely how Luke deals with this tradition and what attitude he adopts toward it, and this question can be answered only if we take Luke and Acts as a single complete work. The very extent of this tradition suggests that we not focus on alterations of detail or on purely formal compositional interventions by Luke. We must expect, rather, that Luke has an overall conception of his own, and we must therefore reckon with compositional interventions that effect, and cannot but effect, a material reworking of the pre-Lucan data in the context of his Gospel.

Moreover, as in dealing with the earliest tradition and with the sayings of the Q group, so in dealing with Luke we must look to the concrete situation of the author and his readers as we try to understand the content of Luke's conception of the social message of the Gospel. Luke's response to social problems, like the responses of the earliest tradition and the wandering prophets, will become unambiguously clear only when seen in the social context of the author himself and of the community he has in view. Only in this way is it possible to understand even supposed contradictions in the Lucan assessment of the social content of the message of Jesus.[5]

If, then, we are to answer our question about the message of Jesus for the poor as seen in Luke, we must, on the one hand, understand the two-part work—Luke and Acts—as projecting the theological conception of its author. We must therefore have recourse to what is called the "redaction-historical" approach to the Gospels. We must, however, broaden this approach to the extent that in dealing with Lucan texts whose origin or pre-Lucan form we can no longer know with accuracy, we try to grasp their meaning in the context of the complete Lucan work and independently of the question of their origin or precise pre-Lucan form. When all is said and done, however, even this modified redaction-historical approach is inadequate for a deeper understanding of Luke. Therefore we must, on the other hand, attempt—since we are inquiring here into the *social* message of Luke—to grasp the concrete historico-social situation of Luke himself or, as the case may be, his community.

At the outset, however, we must as it were cut a path for ourselves through the extensive material Luke provides for the approach we are taking. In the next section, therefore, we shall investigate three somewhat lengthy units of text—Lk. 6:17–49; 12:1–46; 18:18–20—in order to see what Lucan conception emerges from his composition of these units. This will shed light on his position on social problems, especially where we can discern relevant alterations of the pre-Lucan tradition.

II. THE PREACHING OF JESUS TO DISCIPLES AND PEOPLE

1. The Distinction within the Sermon on the Plain (Lk. 6:17–49)

Especially revealing of Luke's contribution is the compositional framework he provides for Jesus' Sermon on the Plain. In this first major discourse by Jesus, Luke distinguishes two groups of addressees: the disciples and the crowd. To this formal distinction correspond material differences in what is said to each group.

The Sermon on the Plain, taken as a whole, contains programmatic statements of Jesus regarding his social message and is therefore extremely important for our analysis. Sizable parts of it undoubtedly come from the tradition that Luke and Matthew share independently of the tradition in Mark and which they derive from the Sayings-source. We need only think, for example, of the Beatitudes and the commandment of love of enemies. In this special case we need not trouble ourselves with an exact reconstruction of the Q tradition behind the sermon and especially with the disputed question of whether the woe-sayings on the rich were already in Q (they are missing from Matthew's Sermon on the Mount).[6]

For the moment we shall consider only the "scenic" setting of the discourse, that is, Lk. 6:17–20a, 27a, and 7:1. Even if elements in it are pre-Lucan, the setting in its Lucan form is the work of the evangelist. He has altered the order of two pericopes that occur one after another in Mark: the healings Jesus works by the lakeside (Mk. 3:7–12) and the calling of the Twelve (Mk. 3:13–19). Luke tells first of the calling (which he evidently regards as important) of twelve disciples to be apostles (Lk. 6:12–16). In his telling of it the choice takes place on a hill that Jesus had ascended with his disciples in order to pray there. After the choice of the apostles, Jesus and his disciples descend the hill again and come to a level field. There a large number of his disciples gather, as does a huge crowd of people from all parts of Judea, from Jerusalem, and even from the non-Jewish coastal region of Tyre and Sidon (Lk. 6:17). Luke thus returns to his model in Mark, but only now, and in the field on the hillside, does he have the healings take place, which in Mark had occurred earlier and by the lakeside. Thus, while using the broad Marcan outline for his Gospel, Luke is able to insert the Sermon on the Plain at this point and thus have it delivered in the presence of those disciples who have already been chosen as apostles.

The discourse of Jesus that begins in Lk. 6:20b is heard by all those who have gathered around him (6:17), that is, by a large number of disciples (*mathētai*; it is not the apostles alone who are meant) and by a huge crowd (*laos*) that probably represents all of Israel and even the pagan world. The discourse of Jesus thus acquires a radical importance from its audience. But, even though all listen, Luke makes a distinction within the Sermon on the Plain. Jesus turns his attention first to his disciples (*mathētai*). He directs his words explicitly to them at the beginning of the discourse and does so in solemn form: "And he lifted his eyes on his disciples and said . . . "(v. 20a). He begins then with the Beatitudes addressed, respectively, to the poor, the hungry, the mourners, and the "persecuted"; in contrast to these Beatitudes are the woe-sayings addressed to the rich, the satiated, the laughers, and those of whom "all men speak well" (vv. 20b–26). As Luke presents the sermon, this part of it is addressed to the disciples of Jesus alone.

The section of the sermon that begins in verse 27b of Luke 6 with the commandment of love of enemies and runs to verse 49 is addressed to the other listeners named in verse 17. Verse 27a ("But I say to you that hear") explicitly introduces this new section of the sermon, while 7:1 indicates its conclusion. Thus, though all present hear everything, the Sermon on the Plain falls into two parts, which are distinguished by their different addressees (disciples and crowd). The distinction is all the more noteworthy in that it is not in the service of some esoteric instruction for the disciples.

The question therefore arises: Why does Luke make this distinction? Why does he expressly set the disciples apart from the crowd? In offering an answer, we must not fail to consider the content that is reserved to the disciples in the part of the sermon addressed to them. Thus the suggestion, for example, that Luke wants the Beatitudes to apply to the disciples as being "the baptized and believing" followers of Jesus is of no help here.[7] The suggestion is useless because, be it noted, nowhere in his two works does Luke say anything about a baptism of the disciples, even though he shows a special interest in baptism. Nor is there any mention of the "faith" of the disciples. If the faith of the disciples is to be the decisive reason why Jesus calls them blessed, it must be because this faith is manifested in the condition here being praised: the condition of poverty.

Yet to be accurate we must modify this statement, for it is not poverty that is praised, but the poor and, specifically, the poor disciples of Jesus. Nor are the disciples poor in a merely metaphorical sense; they are truly poor in an economically definable sense, because on encountering Jesus and deciding to follow him they abandoned everything. Luke alone among the evangelists sets store—and indeed great store—by this total renunciation of possessions on the part of the disciples (and not just the apostles) of Jesus. He says, for example, in connection with the call of Peter and the sons of Zebedee (Lk. 5:1-11), that "when they had brought their boats to land, they left everything (*aphentes panta*) and followed him" (5:11). In the parallel passage of Mark (1:16-20), Simon Peter and his brother Andrew leave "their nets" (v. 18), and the sons of Zebedee leave their father and the "hired servants" (v. 20). It might, of course, be inferred from this that these disciples in fact left everything, but Mark does not say so. Only Luke speaks explicitly of this radical consequence of the following of Jesus. The same thing occurs at the call of Levi, the tax-collector (Mk. 2:13-17 / / Lk. 5:27-32).[8] Here again Luke makes the Marcan text more specific by saying that Levi left everything (Lk. 5:28, *katalipōn panta*); Mark mentions only the fact that Levi followed Jesus, and says nothing about a total renunciation of possessions.

We can hardly fail to see that Luke is concerned to bring out explicitly the complete renunciation of possessions by the disciples of Jesus. It cannot escape the reader of the Gospel, therefore, that by following Jesus his disciples became poor (*ptōchoi*). The way has thus already been prepared for calling them "blessed" because they are poor. But at this point a problem arises. On the one hand, it is not possible to read the entire discourse at the level of the contemporary reader of Luke's Gospel, that is, the community of disciples that is the church.[9] For then we would logically have to suppose that Luke is still requiring from the entire church of his day the voluntary poverty that earned the first disciples of Jesus the appellation *markarioi* ("blessed"). We say "the entire church" because who else in Luke's time would correspond to the crowd whom Jesus addresses in the second part of the sermon? This second part could not be intended for non-Christian outsiders: the commandment of love of enemies could hardly be addressed to them. More importantly, Lk. 6:46— "Why do you call me 'Lord, Lord,' and not do what I tell you?"—supposes that this part of the sermon is likewise addressed to Christians, since the confession of Jesus as Lord (*Kyrios*) can be attributed only to Christians.

On the other hand, the distinction made within the Sermon on the Plain is much too noticeable for us to neglect it when considering the Gospel in relation to the Christians of Luke's day. Consequently, if the discourse in its entirety has the church of Luke in view, the disciples continue to be set apart within it. Scholars have therefore tried to apply the distinction between the addressees of the Sermon on the Plain to the Christians of Luke's day.[10] They say, for example, that in Luke's time a special "class" of Christian officials was meant to apply to itself the first part of the sermon, which is addressed to the disciples. The voluntary poverty of the disciples thus becomes one of the "counsels for perfection" (*consilia evangelica*) that are to be followed only by specially selected Christians.

This interpretation has the advantage that it respects the distinction within the Sermon on the Plain and can give it a meaning in Luke's time. The interpretation breaks down, however, on the fact that in the Acts of the Apostles the title *mathētēs* ("disciple") becomes a synonym for Christians as such (Acts 11:26). Another difficulty is that in Paul's farewell address (Acts

20:17–38) a group of Christians that is evidently set apart has a different title, namely, *presbyteroi* ("elders," v. 17).

In addition, this interpretation tacitly assumes that Luke regards the voluntary poverty of Jesus' disciples as an ideal worth imitating independently of any particular body of practitioners. But the Acts of the Apostles, which tells of the formation of the first Christian communities, says nothing at all of this ideal. Yet in Paul's farewell address to the elders of Ephesus, in which he tells them how to act once he is gone, Luke should certainly have spoken of this ideal if he regarded it as still important. All he says, however, is that the elders, like Paul, should work to support themselves and should look after the "weak." In fact, Luke expects neither the elders nor Christians generally to adopt the voluntary poverty of Jesus' disciples.

This realization should not, however, lead to the view that Luke "historicizes" the ideal of poverty that he finds in earlier Christian tradition. He does assign this poverty to the disciples of a past age, but he nonetheless also gives it a present relevance, even if not in the form of an ethical imitation of this lifestyle.[11] However, it is not possible at this point to make a more detailed application of the disciples' voluntary poverty to the Christians of Luke's day. Before that can be done, we must first examine more fully Luke's presentation of the lifestyle of Jesus' disciples and the function it has for him.

2. Further Evidence of Luke's Distinction (Luke 12)

We have thus far established the fact that in Jesus' Sermon on the Plain, Luke distinguishes between disciples and crowd as two groups of addressees; still undetermined is the present relevance that the part addressed to the disciples may have for the church of Luke. A similar procedure can be seen in Luke 12: here again part of a discourse is addressed to the disciples, part to the crowd. Against the background of the Sermon on the Plain the objective meaning of the differentiation becomes clearer. The dangers inherent in the life of the prosperous and the rich are contrasted with the life of the voluntarily poor disciples of Jesus. Because of their life situation, the disciples receive different admonitions from Jesus than do the rich.

Luke 12:1 depicts an audience situation comparable to that in 6:17. Even though so many "thousands" of people gather that they tread upon one another, Jesus begins by turning first (or "primarily," *prōton*) to his disciples. Luke 12:4 makes it clear that the ensuing exhortation to fearless confession is meant for the disciples, since in that verse Jesus speaks of his friends ("I tell you, my friends"). The huge crowd comes into the picture again only when "one of the multitude" asks him to settle a dispute over an inheritance" (v. 13). And just as Jesus introduced his exhortation to the disciples with the warning: "Beware of the leaven of the Pharisees, which is hypocrisy" (v. 1b), so he precedes his address to the crowd with the warning: "Take heed, and beware of all covetousness" (v. 15). The following story of the foolish rich man (vv. 16–21) serves as a deterrent example of what happens to a person who has succumbed to covetousness (*pleonexia*). Luke 12:13-21 is thus addressed explicitly to the crowd, while vv. 1b-12 are addressed to the disciples. Then, as the introduction in v. 22 shows ("And he said to his disciples"), Luke goes on to draw a special conclusion for the disciples from the story of the foolish rich man. At this point Luke inserts the discourse on anxieties from the Sayings-source (Lk. 12:22ff.).

At this point again, then, a distinction is made between disciples and people, as a special "moral" is drawn from the story of the rich farmer that applies to the disciples and, for the moment, to them alone. Covetousness can no longer be a danger for these men who have left everything. The poor disciples do, however, have problems that are caused by the very opposite of what drives the farmer to covetousness. His superfluity (*perisseuien*) is in contrast with their lack. His precautionary behavior is covetousness; due to their poverty they are in danger of succumbing to a different kind of false "anxiety."

Chapter 12 provides still further evidence of a methodical distinction within the discourses of Jesus as contained in Luke. In 12:41 Peter, representative of the disciples, openly asks: "Lord, are you telling this parable for us or for all?" The question is quite necessary if Luke is to make it clear that Jesus' words on vigilant fidelity (Lk. 12:36ff.) do not apply only to the disciples. Jesus does not answer Peter's question directly, but counters with a question that continues what he has been saying (12:42). It is as though the question were not a question at all but a warning evidently meant for all: Be ready for the coming of the Son of man. In any accounting Peter's question presupposes consciousness of a distinction of addressees in the discourse of Jesus, and in any accounting the differentiation is the work of Luke.

The points made thus far show that, with the help of a simple compositional device, Luke places texts dealing with the problem of poverty and wealth into a context in which a distinction is made. The examples adduced not only show formal correspondences in the scenic settings that Luke provides; in addition they point to the same concrete material intention even when the particular contents differ. Thus the praise of the poor in Jesus' Sermon on the Plain applies only to the disciples of Jesus, not to the rest of the throng, since the disciples have become poor (*ptōchoi*) as part of their following, a point that Luke alone emphasizes. For this very reason, the warning against covetousness with its deterrent example of the rich man cannot apply to the group of disciples but only to the listening throng. For the disciples, who have no possessions, a different moral is drawn from the example: Do not be anxious! Their anxiety about the necessities of life springs quite naturally from the lack of means that their voluntary poverty entails; the blatant precautions of the rich man are in the service of covetousness. Thus the examples chosen from chapters 6 and 12 of Luke also have in common a contrast between rich and poor. Over against the *plousioi* ("rich") of 6:24-26 and 12:13-21 stand the poor disciples of 6:20-23 and 12:1-12, 22ff.

This analysis, of course, presupposes not only that Luke shapes his presentation in a methodical way, but also that he carefully applies the method to details. Is this impression objectively grounded? We shall use the Lucan version of the story of the "rich young man" (Lk. 18:18–30//Mk. 10:17–31) to test the results thus far obtained and to extend them. The text is an obvious choice because our knowledge of the model for this story in Mark allows us to see exactly where and how Luke altered and interpreted it.

3. The Story of the "Rich Young Man" (Lk. 18:18–30//Mk. 10:17–31)

The story of a rich man whose possessions keep him from accepting Jesus' call to discipleship is taken by Luke from the Gospel of Mark. A comparison of the Lucan version of the story with the model in Mark yields detailed knowledge of the way Luke works. True enough, if we look at the two pericopes in isolation, the results of such a synoptic comparison will seem rather meager, and we shall judge the changes Luke makes in his Marcan model to be trifling. If, however, we keep in mind the foregoing analysis of Luke, it becomes clear that even minor alterations made by Luke contribute to a serious change in the whole thrust of the story. In fact, Luke proposes his own interpretation of it, giving the pericope a new function and different meaning in the context of his Gospel.

The story as told by Mark can be readily divided into two parts. The first is the tale of a wealthy man whose possessions keep him from accepting the call of Jesus to discipleship (Mk. 10:17–22). The second is an ensuing conversation between Jesus and his disciples on the man's refusal of the call (Mk. 10:23–31).

Luke does not retain this structure. The change of scene in Mark, which is occasioned by the rich man's departure, does not take place in Luke, because here the rich ruler (archōn) does not leave the place of the action. Instead, Jesus' sad comment on the difficulty the rich have in entering the basileia tou Theou ("kingdom of God") is uttered to the rich man himself, whereas in Mark it opens the discussion with the disciples.

In Mark the disciples interrupt Jesus' lament from time to time with their reactions. First, they show amazement at the idea that the rich should have difficulty entering the basileia. Jesus therefore continues in more general terms, bewailing the fact that it is difficult for anyone at all to enter the kingdom of God. This lament is followed by the "camel-saying," according to which it is easier for a camel to pass through the eye of a needle than for a rich man to enter the basileia. At this harsh saying of Jesus the disciples are startled and ask one another, "Then who can be saved?" Finally, Jesus answers this question by leaving to the grace of God this humanly impossible feat.

Luke has the rich ruler present during the conversation about the difficulty of entering the kingdom of God, and he passes over the reactions of the disciples. The very lament of Jesus has a different look here. In addition, Luke gives the whole story a different thrust. The rich man is introduced as a high-ranking personage (an archōn). As Luke's correction (Lk. 18:23) of his Marcan model shows—"He was plousious sphodra ("very rich")—he is explicitly concerned to provide a "sociological" characterization of this man as a high-ranking and wealthy individual. The description determines the course of the story.

The ruler asks Jesus what he must do in order to inherit eternal life. Jesus refers to the commandments; the ruler has kept these from his youth. Jesus then says to him, "One thing you still lack. Sell all that you have and distribute to the poor, and you will have treasure in heaven; and come, follow me" (Lk. 18:22). At this demand the ruler becomes "very sad" (*perilypos*), "for he was very rich." Still gazing at the rich man, Jesus immediately says, "How hard it is for those who have riches to enter the kingdom of God! For it is easier for a camel to go through the eye of a needle than for a rich man to enter the kingdom of God" (vv. 24f.). Not only, then, does Luke omit the reaction of the disciples, but he also omits the generalized statement of the difficulty of entering the *basileia*. Finally, in Luke it is not the disciples but an audience introduced by him that asks, "Then who can be saved?"

It would certainly be insufficient to assume that Luke's presentation necessarily takes the form it does because he has the rich man present throughout. For he could, in theory, have had the whole Marcan conversation between Jesus and the disciples take place in the presence of the rich man. The fact is that it makes complete sense for Luke to have Jesus address the rich man and to leave the disciples out of it. Why? Because in Luke's Gospel it is no longer possible for the disciples of Jesus to wonder that the wealthy should have difficulty entering the *basileia* or to be startled that such an entrance seems obviously impossible. Furthermore, in the context of Luke's Gospel the question of who can be saved is likewise impossible in the mouths of the disciples. We shall go into these points in detail.

The first point to note is that the story of the rich ruler is the story of an unsuccessful call to discipleship. The demand made by Jesus—"Sell everything and follow me"—is a call to follow him as a disciple. This element is already present in Mark, of course, but in Luke the call to become a *mathētēs* ("disciple") has a very distinctive meaning, since for him, as we have already seen, the complete renunciation of possessions is part of the following of Jesus. It is not accidental, therefore, that when Jesus bids the rich man sell his possessions, Luke should clarify the demand by adding a *panta* ("all") that is not in his Marcan model. Unlike Mark, Luke had already altered the story of the call of Peter, the sons of Zebedee, and Levi by having them leave everything to follow Jesus (Lk. 5:11, 28). Two other verses make it clear in addition that in Luke's view the complete renunciation of possessions is a constitutive part of the following of Jesus as a disciple. In Lk. 12:33—and again only in Luke— Jesus calls for this renunciation: "Sell your possessions, and give [the proceeds as] alms"; the context makes it clear that this exhortation is addressed solely to the disciples of Jesus. The same demand is made in Lk. 14:33, in a context in which Jesus is setting down the conditions for following him as a disciple: "So therefore, whoever of you does not renounce all that he has cannot be my disciple." This verse too is special to Luke. It is therefore beyond doubt that in Luke's eyes a complete renunciation of possessions is an indispensable consequence of following Jesus as his disciple.

We must, however, advance a step further in the argument if we are to understand Luke's interpretation of the story of the rich ruler. Up to this point it has become clear only that complete renunciation of possessions is part of life as a disciple and that the story of the rich ruler is the story of an unsuccessful call to a rich man to become a disciple. Still not yet fully explained are the changes Luke makes in Jesus' lament over the difficulty, indeed the sheer impossibility of the propertied or rich to enter the kingdom of God.

The explanation of these changes is to be found in another peculiarity in Luke's development of the theme of discipleship: the call of Jesus to a following as a disciple is always a call to the present kingdom of God. To those who accept the call and the consequences it entails, Jesus promises a share in the *basileia* here and now: "Blessed are you poor, for yours is (*estin*) the kingdom of God" (Lk. 6:20b). And in the discourse to the disciples regarding "anxieties," Luke says, "Fear not, little flock, for it is your Father's good pleasure to give (*dounai*) you the kingdom" (Lk. 12:32). Finally, as Luke's interpretation of discipleship in the story of the rich ruler shows, the disciples have left everything for the sake of the kingdom of God. Account must also be taken here of the much discussed answer of Jesus—"Behold, the kingdom of God is in the midst of you (*entos hymōon estin*)" (Lk. 17:21)—to the Pharisees' question about when the *basileia* is coming.

This last answer of Jesus in Luke also enables us to understand how the evangelist represents the present reign of God. The kingdom is present in the person of Jesus, just as the power or rule of a secular *basileia* is present in the person of the emperor or other head of state or his representative. Jesus' call to discipleship is a call to the present kingdom, a kingdom that (to put the matter in cautious terms) is present on earth with Jesus. *That* is the call issued to the rich ruler, and that is the call he rejects.

Finally, this interpretation of Luke is further confirmed by a seemingly insignificant change, which the evangelist introduces into his Marcan model. In Mark Jesus regretfully says how difficult it is for the wealthy to enter the future kingdom of God ("enter," *eiseleusontai*, Mk. 10:23, is in the future tense). In Luke, however, Jesus speaks of this difficulty as applying to the present ("enter," *eisporeuontai*, Lk. 18:24, is in the present tense). The Lucan Jesus thus says nothing about the heavenly future of the rich ruler, but only about his present or, rather, the present of the kingdom of God. It is now, in the presence of Jesus and therefore in the presence of the kingdom of God, that the ruler rejects the following of Jesus and his own share in the kingdom. He thus makes himself an example of the woe pronounced upon the rich. The poor disciples of Jesus are declared blessed because they share in the present kingdom of God. A woe is pronounced upon the rich because they have already received their "consolation" (*paraklēsis*) (Lk. 6:20b, 24).

The rich ruler knows and observes the commandments, but he is unwilling to heed the command that the hour imposes on him: "Sell everything and follow me." The woe pronounced upon the rich—and expressed here in the form of the camel-saying—applies therefore to him because he does not enter the present *basileia*. Can it be accidental that Luke omits the "emotional" reaction of Jesus found in Mark: "Jesus looking upon him loved him" (Mk. 10:21)? Such a reaction is hardly compatible with the woe-saying that is verified in this man who does not enter the kingdom of God because he clings to his wealth.

The Lucan interpretation seems also to influence the answer Jesus gives to the question of the hearers: "Then who can be saved?" In Mark Jesus states categorically: "With men it is impossible," and then allows that it is possible with God (Mk. 10:27). The Lucan Jesus is not so categorical, but speaks in more general terms: "What is impossible with men is possible with God" (Lk. 18:26). For are not the disciples here present a living counterproof that it is possible for human beings to be saved? Peter, speaking as representative of the disciples, goes on to make the same point: "Lo, we have left our homes and followed you" (Lk. 18:28). Luke is here again following Mark's outline of the story, but in his version it is here that the disciples speak for the first time. Peter's statement allows us to infer that Luke here again chooses to emphasize temporality (both grammatically, as it were, and objectively). He depicts the following by the disciples as a now completed event that took place at a moment in the past (*ekolouthesamen,* aorist tense), whereas Mark uses the perfect tense (*ekolouthekamen*) and describes it as a state that lasts into the present.[12]

Finally, Luke also omits the concluding saying in Mark: "But many that are first will be last, and the last first" (Mk. 10:31).[13] In the context of the conversation with the disciples that has taken place after the departure of the rich young man, Mark uses this "eschatological question mark" to criticize the self-important reference of Peter to the renunciation that the disciples have made. Luke, on the other hand, casts no doubt on the renunciation of the disciples, even from an eschatological standpoint. These men do have a share in the *basileia,* and they have it even now. Luke's omission of this verse lends further support to our hypothesis that he has a very definite picture of discipleship, of the poverty that is part of it, and of the disciples' present share in the reign of God. To this picture corresponds an equally definite assessment of the rich. Therefore, voluntary poverty, being a disciple of Jesus, and present participation in the kingdom of God all go together, just as riches prevent discipleship and the rich are excluded from the present *basileia*.

III. WHAT IS THE SIGNIFICANCE OF THE DISCIPLES' VOLUNTARY POVERTY?

1. The Poverty of the Disciples as Something of the Past, Belonging to the Lifetime of Jesus

It has been our intention to gain access to the social message of Luke. In what way do the preceding analyses help to this end?

We began by showing that a striking distinction in formal setting exists in two discourses of Jesus that are relevant to our concern. Luke distinguishes between the disciples and the crowd as addressees of Jesus' message. To the disciples he addresses his praise of the poor, while he addresses to the crowd the part of the Sermon on the Plain that begins with the commandment of love of enemies. He reminds the crowd of the danger of covetousness, but for the disciples he draws a different lesson from the behavior of the rich farmer.

This formal distinction is matched by a distinction of content. The Beatitude of the poor is addressed to the disciples, because in following Jesus they have voluntarily become poor. The Lucan Jesus praises neither poverty as such nor individuals who are unwillingly condemned to poverty. In Luke's view poverty as a consequence of the voluntary renunciation of possessions is a price that must unconditionally be paid for following Jesus as a disciple.

On the other hand, and as a result, the warning against covetousness is no longer applicable to the disciples. Their problem is not the possession of superfluities and the resultant danger of making covetous provision for the future but, rather, the lack of necessities and the resultant danger of becoming anxious about bare subsistence rather than anxious first of all for the reign of God.

The unsuccessful call of the rich ruler then serves as confirmation that Jesus is right in pronouncing woe upon the rich and that voluntary poverty is part of life as a disciple. On the one hand, in the programmatic Sermon on the Plain the poor disciples are called blessed and are rewarded with participation in the already present *basileia*; on the other hand, woe is pronounced in principle upon the rich because they remain excluded from the kingdom of God, at least in the kingdom as now present. For this reason Luke quite logically removes any trace of sympathy with the rich from the story of the rich ruler, while at the same time he rejects any attempt to cast doubt on the achievement of the disciples and its reward.

We saw next that in the context of the problem of discipleship, statements about the voluntary poverty of Jesus' disciples are closely linked to statements about the rich. Complete renunciation of possessions, the following of Jesus as disciples, and participation in the present reign of God are immediately connected with one another and are contrasted with statements about the rich who, as represented by the ruler, reject the call to discipleship because of their wealth and are therefore excluded from the reign of God.

This linking of the two types of statement could be understood to mean that Luke makes discipleship the point of reference for the problem of poverty and wealth. In this supposition he would be emphasizing the stubborn hold on wealth as much as he does simply because the voluntary poverty of the disciples emerges all the more clearly by contrast. Finally, Luke leaves no doubt that the following of Jesus as disciples is a thing of the past. This suggests that in Luke's view the social gulf between poor and rich is also a problem belonging to the past.

Luke undoubtedly does understand the following of Jesus as disciples to be a phenomenon of the past. That is, he depicts the following of Jesus' disciples in such a way that contemporary readers of the Gospel are very unlikely to think they, as Christians, must follow Jesus in the same way as the disciples did in their day. "Very unlikely" because a key condition for the possibility of that kind of following is no longer verified: Jesus is no longer on earth. It is precisely Luke who highlights this change by the story of the ascension of Jesus, which marks the end of his earthly activity and the beginning of his heavenly state of readiness to assist us (see Lk. 24:50-53; Acts 1:1-11; 2:33-36). This change in the presence of Jesus and consequently of God's reign is matched by a change in the "function" of the disciples of Jesus. They are now to be witnesses to the destiny (and especially the resurrection) of Jesus as foretold in the Scriptures and to preach conversion for the forgiveness of sins to all peoples (Lk. 24:44-49; Acts 1:8). This new function of the disciple-apostle is brought out once again in the by-election of Matthias as an apostle (Acts 1:22). This is the last occasion on which we glimpse the great crowd of Jesus' disciples, who form a reserve supply of witnesses (Acts 1:21f.); after this we hear no more of them. Finally, even within the Gospel and therefore during the lifetime of Jesus, Luke makes temporal distinctions. In Lk. 22:35-38 Jesus looks back to earlier sendings of the disciples and makes it clear that a new period of their lives is now beginning.

Does Luke see the problem posed by the rich as likewise something past, something that disappeared with the kind of possession-free discipleship practiced in the days of Jesus' earthly ministry? The idea would be, for instance, that in the time of Jesus voluntary poverty was the need of the hour, and wealth was the great bar to entrance into the kingdom of God. Today, however (in the time of the Lucan community), no one can any longer follow Jesus to Jerusalem; as a result, not only is this specific form of following outdated, but the problem of wealth must also be seen differently.

We cannot list here the variations on this kind of "historicizing" interpretation of Luke's approach to the problem of the poor and the rich.[14] All of them have in common the undoubtedly correct insight that in Luke the complete renunciation of possessions has for its context the following of Jesus during the latter's lifetime. They fail to realize, however, that although the voluntary poverty of the disciples is now a thing of the past, it continues to have a present meaning. Luke is not a "pastor to the rich" in the sense that he regards the criticism of them found in the earliest Jesus tradition as a phenomenon of the past.

For the moment, however, we must set aside the question of the present meaning of criticism of the rich, because the problem of the now past renunciation of possessions by the disciples calls for closer examination. The reason is that the meaning of "past" in this context is still an unresolved question. In order to answer it we must look more carefully at the special way in which Luke presents the life of the disciples of Jesus. As we have already seen, Luke's attention is focused on the voluntary poverty of these disciples and on their participation in the present *basileia*. Luke undoubtedly has a special interest in the complete renunciation of possessions by the disciples of Jesus; this is clear from the emphasis that he alone of the evangelists places on it. To this end he makes use of the scanty data in Mark and, with the help of the Sayings-source, paints a highly personal picture of the life of the disciples. In the next section we shall examine this picture to the extent that it is relevant to our investigation into the social message of Luke. The primary question to be answered is what meaning this now past way of life of the disciples has for the present thrust of Luke's social message.

2. The Simple Life of the Disciples as a Literary Ideal

Why does Luke, and strictly speaking Luke alone, emphasize the fact that the disciples of Jesus leave everything in following him? The point to be kept in mind from the outset is that according to Luke the first disciples of Jesus voluntarily make themselves poor (ptōchoi). They are not born poor, nor are they forced into poverty by their economic situation. Their poverty is the result of a complete renunciation of possessions. It is therefore depicted not as a deplorable condition but as behavior appropriate for disciples. Luke is therefore not glorifying poverty that is simply endured. In his Gospel, ptōchoi in that sense applies only to those who receive "alms," and not to the disciples of Jesus. The voluntarily poor disciples and those whom destiny has beggared are connected in Luke only inasmuch as the latter profit by the renunciation of the former (Lk. 12:33; 18:22). In Luke it is not the poor whom Jesus calls to be disciples, but those who have possessions that can be abandoned or sold.[15] True enough, they are all ordinary folk (fishermen, tax collectors)—except for the rich ruler, but his call is not effective—but they are not destitute.

A first answer, then, to the question why Luke so emphasizes the voluntary poverty of the disciples must be that their poverty is a literary ideal in Luke. That we are indeed in the presence of a literary ideal is clear from the fact that Luke cannot think of the disciples of Jesus as involuntarily poor; he can only picture their poverty as resulting from a respectable renunciation.

There is a passage in Luke's Gospel that makes his outlook vividly clear; it is 22:35-38, where he again speaks of the mission of the disciples. He who has a purse or a bag is now to take it with him. He who has no sword is to sell his himation ("mantle") and buy one. Now, as we saw when examining the missionary discourse in the Sayings-source, a himation was almost prohibitively expensive for the average Jewish citizen, that is, the ordinary folk of Palestine, in the time of Jesus. Such a mantle would have cost a day laborer a half-year's pay. Clearly, then, Luke deals in a rather cavalier fashion with one of the most valuable possessions of the ordinary folk of Palestine. This detail brings out both the literary nature of Luke's picture of life as a disciple and the evangelist's own social background.

Great caution must therefore be exercised in drawing conclusions from Luke's accounts of the way of life of Jesus' disciples about the historical situation of the Palestinian followers of Jesus in the second third of the first century. Gerd Theissen has attempted to sum up the situation of these disciples of Jesus in the term "vagabond radicalism."[16] It is to passages in Luke that Theissen turns for evidence of this phenomenon of social uprooting. In fact, we may generalize and say that passages in Luke are the basis of important components in Theissen's picture of the wandering charismatics who, he says, appeared on the Palestinian scene as disciples of Jesus in the second third of the first century. This is true especially of what Theissen calls the "ethos" of "life without possessions" and also (as he subsequently makes clear) the "afamilial ethos" of these vagabond radicals. When discussing the Sayings-source we showed that the historical situation of the wandering charismatics as presented by Theissen was largely the situation of the Q prophets, but that the picture he draws of these radicals did not represent the Q prophets. Now we can say that Theissen's picture of the lifestyle of the vagabond radicals largely corresponds to Luke's picture of the disciples, but the historical situation in which he locates his radicals is not that of Luke's disciples.

Luke's picture of the poverty of the disciples has been influenced by extra-biblical literary ideals. This statement must, however, not be misinterpreted. Luke is not, for example, reveling in happy reminiscences of the heroic beginnings of the Christian movement and praising a past time when it was still possible for disciples to throw away encumbering possessions and devote their lives wholly to Jesus or, subsequently, the preaching of the gospel. He does not share the yearning of prosperous and educated Hellenists of his day, who dreamed of the simple life in which hunger is the best cook, work the best sleeping pill, and bodily stamina gained by toughening the best doctor. The enthusiasts for that kind of simple life, supposedly lived in the dim past or by primitive peoples or by groups still largely untouched by civilization, were to be found among men like Seneca, a rich landowner, or Dion of Prusa, an orator and cultural critic, or Virgil, court poet to Augustus.[17]

No, Luke does not depict the poor life of Jesus' disciples as idyllic or as the comfortable existence held up for imitation to a decadent upper class grown weary of culture and luxury. He does not turn the simple life of the disciples into a call back to nature or into a rich man's daydream in which the hard life of the poor is contrasted with a life increasingly burdened by anxiety and greed. There is indeed much in the picture of Jesus' disciples that reminds us of the ideal of the simple life in Greek and Roman literature; nonetheless the voluntary poverty of Jesus' disciples in Luke is not an ideal that would delight and charm the rich. After all, the poverty of the disciples is paired with pitiless woe-sayings about the rich. Finally, as we have already pointed out, this form of discipleship has for its irretrievable and unreproducible context the following of Jesus on the road to Jerusalem, and Luke nowhere isolates the discipleship from this special closeness to Jesus, nowhere gives it an independent meaning as an ideal worth imitating.

As a matter of fact, the only reason for the disciples' complete renunciation of possessions in Luke is their extraordinary encounter with Jesus. That is how the matter is represented in the Lucan vocation stories (5:1-11, 27-32), in which Jesus does not explicitly ask for such a renunciation. Even Lk. 12:33–34 gives no ethical reason for the renunciation: "Sell your possessions, and give alms; provide yourselves with purses that do not grow old, with a treasure in the heavens that does not fail, where no thief approaches and no moth destroys. For where your treasure is, there will your heart be also." This exhortation is addressed to the disciples, for Luke characteristically omits in this context the prohibition: "Do not lay up for yourselves treasures on earth" (Mt. 6:19a). Instead of this warning about the transiency of possessions, Luke has an incomparably more radical call for the selling of them. He has no interest in warning against *thēsaurizein* ("treasure-gathering") and therefore avoids the concept in Lk. 12:33b (unlike Mt. 6:20). Everything is subordinated here to the following of Jesus as his disciples. In other words, Lk. 12:33 is not an ethical exhortation but describes the concrete consequence of discipleship while Jesus is still present on earth.

A glance at Lk. 14:25–33, where Jesus lists the conditions he requires of a disciple, makes the situation unmistakably clear. He is on the road, and a large crowd of people is following him. He now explains to the crowd the extraordinary demands made of a disciple. A disciple is not simply one who travels the roads with Jesus; he must in addition make uncompromising and radical renunciations. As the movement of the pericope makes clear, the supreme demand is the complete renunciation of possessions. This is emphasized by being placed at the end.

Two preceding comparisons—the building of a tower and the conduct of a war—already bring out the exceptional extent of the demands made. There is no need of pushing the comparisons too far, since their point is immediately clear: a great enterprise requires that we consider the costs and decide whether we have the stamina to see it through. The comparisons tell us: Weigh the consequences! Realize what a vast undertaking you are planning![18] These generalizations are made concrete for discipleship by the explicit conditions that Jesus sets down, culminating in the complete renunciation of possessions.

Luke does not establish a rational, "logical" series of requirements. To the healthy mind, the demand that disciples should "hate" their own life and should, if need be, even sacrifice it as a martyr on the cross (Lk. 14:26f.) will make the renunciation of possessions seem a feat of the second rank, since life is the supreme good. Yet Luke does not adopt this rational sequence and present the surrender of life as the climactic renunciation.[19] Instead, in his version of discipleship, the renunciation of possessions is the supreme demand made on the follower of Jesus. This inference from our observations on Lk. 14:25–33 is confirmed by the story of the unsuccessful call to the rich ruler.

3. The Poverty of the Disciples as a Critique of the Rich

What is the real function of this literary ideal in Luke? Until now no answer has presented itself. Our answer is that the renunciation of Jesus' disciples, with the voluntary renunciation of possessions as its highest manifestation, has the function of a critique of the rich.

We pointed out earlier that even in the drawing rooms of wealthy houses people dreamed of the simple life. Admittedly, it was probably a rare event for one of these dreamers to think of actually adopting the simple life. This is true at bottom even in Epictetus' discourse on the extremely plain life of the Cynics.[20]

In this discourse Epictetus meets an acquaintance who is evidently inclined to try following the Cynic ideal, and Epictetus therefore paints a picture for him of the model Cynic hero. Epictetus leaves no doubt about the fact that he himself has not adopted this kind of simple life and that at this period those who claim to be Cynics do not embody in even the smallest degree the Cynic ideal of a Crates or a Diogenes. "True" Cynics like Crates and Diogenes no longer exist. Epictetus himself as it were transforms Cynic ideals into Stoic ideals. Thus while the Cynics call for the renunciation of possessions, Epictetus expects, rather, that possessions will be regarded as something "indifferent" (*adiaphoron*), which one is to use as though one did not possess it at all. His primary concern is with the "spiritual" attitude of the possessor and not with the mere fact of possession. He is able nonetheless to speak in glowing terms of the heroic renunciations of the Cynics, and he points to the lives of Crates and Diogenes as models for those desiring to call themselves Cynics.

Here again a nonbiblical example shows that ethical radicalism did not necessarily find its concrete expression solely in the lifestyle of vagabond radicals. One could, like Epictetus, talk of this radicalism in the schools of philosophy and meanwhile live well on the fees paid by the auditors.

The lifestyle of the wandering Cynic philosophers nonetheless provides the closest literary parallel to the picture Luke gives of the life of the disciples. We refer not to Epictetus' reinterpretation of the genuine Cynic life, but to the faithful portrayal of that life insofar as this can still be found in Epictetus. There is, of course, no question even in Luke of identifying the disciples of Jesus with the wandering Cynic philosophers; the two groups can, however, be profitably compared. In the light of this comparison we can then answer our question about the significance that the specific lifestyle of Jesus' disciples in Luke has for the latter's message to his contemporaries.

The life lived by Jesus' disciples has two characteristics to which Luke alone gives prominence and which call for a comparison with the wandering Cynic philosophers. These are the complete renunciation of possessions, already mentioned, and the forsaking of wives. Luke 18:29f. and 14:26 speak of leaving wives. Luke 18:29f. says: " . . . there is no man who has left house or wife or brothers or parents or children, for the sake of the kingdom of God, who will not receive manifold more in this time, and in the age to come eternal life." The model for these two verses in Mark (10:29f.) had not mentioned wives. Again, in listing the conditions for discipleship, Lk. 14:26 says: "If any one comes to me and does not hate his own father and mother and wife and children and brothers and sisters, yes, and even his own life, he cannot be my disciple." The corresponding verse in Matthew says simply: "He who loves father or mother more than me is not worthy of me; and he who loves son or daughter more than me is not worthy of me" (Mt. 10:37). Here Luke again adds "wives," while at the same time he makes the entire formulation more radical and comprehensive and relates the demands explicitly to the life of the disciples. The concept *misein* ("hate"), which Luke uses in this context, is to be understood here (as 18:29f. shows) to mean the termination of a communion. It is not an expression of feeling, as it is for us.

It is to be observed in this connection that Luke has his own views regarding the Christians of his community and their relation to their wives. Like Paul he seems to regard celibacy as an ideal recommended to all Christians. There is an indication of this in, for example, the specifically Lucan version of the story in which the Sadducees question Jesus about the resurrection. When asked which of seven brothers will, at the resurrection, possess the wife whom all of them married on earth in order that their brother might have a posterity, Jesus answers, in Luke's version: "The sons of this age marry and are given in marriage; but those who are accounted worthy to attain to that age and to the resurrection from the dead neither marry nor are given in marriage" (Lk. 20:34f.). In the Marcan model for this passage the celibacy in question applies solely to the future resurrection (Mk. 12:25). Luke is not referring to the disciples of Jesus because they are not faced with the question of marrying or not marrying, but must abandon their wives; Lk. 20:34f. is perhaps to be understood as analogous with 1 Corinthians 7. Also in favor of our interpretation is the fact that among the excuses given for not attending the great banquet, Luke alone has a man say that he has married and therefore cannot come (14:20). Finally, Luke also has an unusual formulation of the prohibition against divorce: it forbids the remarriage of divorced persons or, to put it differently, it forbids divorce insofar as it is followed by remarriage (see 16:18). Does Luke mean that Christians may not dissolve existing marriages if they are going to marry again, but that those not yet married should remain celibate?

In any case, the complete separation from wives has nothing to do either with celibacy as a universal Christian ideal or with divorce and remarriage. It remains a hallmark of the exceptional lifestyle of the disciples. The separation from wives is also different from voluntary celibacy; that is, it is not to be understood by analogy with the choice made by Paul who, though he had the right to take a sister with him as a wife, preferred to remain celibate (see 1 Cor. 9:5). Luke makes a more radical demand of the disciples of Jesus: They *must* abandon their wives, thus even dissolving existing marriages. In fact, they must renounce all the family ties that people take for granted.

The special traits in Luke's picture of the life of the disciples justify a comparison with the situation of the Cynics. In the discourse mentioned earlier, Epictetus discusses at length the question whether or not a Cynic should marry and have children. He argues for the celibacy of the Cynic and indeed for a completely afamilial attitude on the Cynic's part. A Cynic may not marry because he should be "undistracted entirely, devoted to the service of God, able to go to and fro among men, not tied down to acts which befit private occasions (*idiōtikos*), nor involved in personal relations."[21] The concerns and duties that the father of a family has toward wife and children would inevitably keep him from his duties as a Cynic. He breaks the bonds holding him to a small human community because the whole of humankind has been entrusted to him.

Epictetus goes on to ask: "How is it possible for a man who has nothing (*mēden echonta*), naked, without home or hearth, in squalor, without a slave, without a city, to live a tranquil life?" Diogenes gives the answer: "Look at me, I have no house or city, property or slave: I sleep on the ground, I have no wife or children, no miserable palace, but only earth and sky and one poor cloak."[22] Thus the lack of possessions is characteristic of the Cynic, no less than is celibacy and an afamilial outlook generally. Like the discourses of Epictetus, the collection of sayings compiled by Diogenes Laertius (*Lives of Eminent Philosophers*) contains accounts of the renunciation of possessions, which the Cynics practiced as an example to others. We are told of Crates in particular that

> he turned his property into money—for he belonged to a distinguished family—and having thus collected about 200 talents, distributed that sum among his fellow-citizens. . . . Diocles relates how Diogenes per-suaded Crates to give up his fields to sheep pasture, and throw into the sea any money he had. . . . Demetrius of Magnesia tells a story that he [Crates] entrusted a banker with a sum of money on condition that, if his sons proved ordinary men, he was to pay it to them, but, if they became philosophers, then to distribute it among the people: for his sons would need nothing, if they took to philosophy.[23]

A Hellenistic reader would immediately have thought of the wandering Cynic philosophers when he came upon Luke's picture of the lifestyle of the disciples of Jesus. Later on, Lucian in his *Peregrinus* tells of a wandering Cynic preacher who was able to pass effortlessly from Christian groups to the Cynic camp.[24] The entire lifestyle of the disciples of Jesus, as described by Luke, might well be understood as comparable to the utterly modest lifestyle of the Cynics. The disciples renounce their possessions, break all the ties that bind human beings together in community, wander from place to place, engage in healing and preaching, and enter homes in order to preach and heal therein. If they find no accommodations, they must sleep in the open, being worse off in this respect than the foxes and the birds. Even their garb resembles that of the Cynics in being utterly unassuming. Their own lives mean nothing to them.[25]

This far-reaching analogy between the life of the disciples of Jesus and the life of the Cynics can be of help to us in the question of the meaning that the voluntary poverty of the disciples has. For the poor and utterly modest lifestyle of the authentic Cynic served above all as a penetrating criticism of wealth and the luxury of the rich.[26] This critical orientation of the Cynic way of life controls what is said on the subject in the dialogue *Cynicus* of Pseudo-Lucian, which was mentioned earlier.

Pseudo-Lucian's Cynicus brings his message, of which his lifestyle is a constitutive part, to sensible rich people. He goes barefoot, wears only a coarse cloak, and makes his bed on the hard ground; a lifestyle that resembles that of the beasts of the forest more than anything else sets him completely apart from other people. And yet he does not adopt this way of life as an alternative to the life of society as a whole; his aim is, rather, to be a living criticism of a culture that takes its tone from the rich with their wasteful luxury. The rich are carried away by passions, thirst for glory, and desire for gain, just as a rider is carried away by a wild horse. Cynicus offers his own way of life and his message as an exhortation and warning against this lifestyle of the rich. He wants to bring understanding; he seeks out therefore those of the rich who still value virtue. In one way his program is quite ambitious, for it is a criticism of society. To a sensible rich man he says:

> You don't think your own land and sea adequate, but import your pleasures from the ends of the earth, you always prefer the exotic to the home-produced, the costly to the inexpensive, what is hard to obtain to what is easy. . . . Consider how much they cost. . . . in blood, death and destruction for mankind, not only because many men are lost at sea for the sake of these things, and suffer terribly in searching for them abroad or manufacturing them at home, but also because they are bitterly fought for, and for them you lay plots against one another, friends against friends, children against fathers, and wives against husbands.[27]

It is to this antisocial way of life that Cynicus opposes his own unassuming way of life as an extreme alternative. The lifestyle and message of this Cynicus (a literary figure in which the message and way of life of real Cynics is summed up in heightened form) are a substantial critique of the rich. Cynicus does not call upon anyone to imitate him, but turns his life into a message attacking the luxurious and antisocial manner of life that is so perilous for the rich themselves.

The Lucan picture of the simple life of Jesus' disciples is to be understood in precisely the same way. In particular, the voluntary poverty that the disciples have embraced as a result of their renunciation of possessions contradicts the behavior of the rich in a way that could hardly be bettered. And the opposition is not limited to the rich who clung to their wealth in the time of Jesus' earthly ministry and were unable to fulfill the command of the hour. Rather, the disciples' life of poverty has the same meaning also, and especially, for Luke's own time. For this poverty is not only the nucleus of their discipleship; it is also in stark contradiction to the life of the foolish rich farmer (Luke 12). In other words, the picture given of the voluntary poverty of Jesus' disciples does not have for its sole function to underscore their renunciation of possessions. On the contrary, Luke emphasizes this particular renunciation because it serves as a critique and warning for the rich of his own day.

As a matter of fact, the voluntary poverty of the disciples is but one aspect (though an aspect that is broadly developed) of a more comprehensive theme in Luke: his uncompromising critique of the rich. Luke has such a great interest in the poverty of the disciples because he is preoccupied to an extraordinary degree with criticizing the rich, and specifically the rich Christians of his own time. This preoccupation gives the voluntary poverty of the disciples its relevance for Luke's time. This point will be developed in the next section. Later on we shall turn to the question of Luke's positive social program.

IV. THE PERILOUS LIFE OF RICH CHRISTIANS

1. The Rich and Respected as Addressees of the Social Message of Jesus

The central themes in the message of Jesus according to Luke are the concern of Jesus for "sinners" and his "good news for the poor." Both themes have their place in our investigation. For, as will be seen, Jesus is contrasted, as "Savior of sinners," with those who despise sinners, and the good news to the poor serves as an admonition to the rich.

The picture of Jesus as savior of sinners is given programmatic expression in Luke in the interpretation of Jesus' "mission": "I have not come to call the righteous, but sinners to repentance" (5:32).[28] Jesus makes this statement in the house of Levi, the tax collector recently called to be a disciple, and in response to the reproach that he or his disciples, as the case may be, sit at table with tax collectors and sinners. It is to be noted that to this saying of Jesus as transmitted in Mark, Luke adds "to repentance" (eis metanoian). Jesus therefore calls the despised with the aim of moving them to repentance.

Who are these despised individuals? In Luke they are exemplified by the tax collectors. And yet these people were not among the poor in the economic sense of this word. Levi, for example, has something to renounce, and he gives a farewell dinner in his home. And yet as a tax collector he is among those whom society despises. In other words, in this special instance the individual is not only one of the ordinary people (like artisans, fishermen, etc.), but in addition is suspect, by reason of his profession, of engaging in illegal activities (see Lk. 3:12f.).

From this point of view the rich chief tax collector, Zacchaeus, is on the same level as the low-ranking tax gatherer, Levi, who in theory could have been the former's employee and far removed from him in economic status. For this rich chief tax collector is likewise called a harmatōlos ("sinner," Lk. 19:7).

Yet it is precisely these despised individuals (both Levi and Zacchaeus) whose guest Jesus becomes, and he even calls Levi to be one of his disciples. The reason given for Jesus' behavior to Zacchaeus—"For the Son of man came to seek and to save the lost" (Lk. 19:10)—resembles that given in Lk. 5:32 for his behavior to Levi. His concern for tax collectors and sinners is a concern for those whom society despises. These individuals may be simply ordinary people, as in the case of the call issued to Peter and the sons of Zebedee (Lk. 5:1-11); they may be ordinary folk who, as in the case of Levi the tax collector, have a reputation for illegal dealings; they may be rich folk who, as in the case of Zacchaeus, a wealthy chief tax collector, are nonetheless in bad repute because of their occupation.

Over against all these people stand the respected members of society; in Luke these are represented chiefly by the Pharisees. The latter "murmur" at Jesus' concern for the despised. They do so on occasion of the farewell meal in the home of Levi (Lk. 5:30), and again at the beginning of Luke 15: "Now the tax collectors and sinners were all drawing near to him. And the Pharisees and the scribes murmured, saying, 'This man receives sinners and eats with them.' "

In the three following parables involving lost objects, the theme is the joy of recovery. Like the brother who remains behind in the parable of the lost son, the Pharisees and scribes are urged to join in the rejoicing at the sinner's conversion (Lk. 15:7, 10, 32).[29] The contrast between the respected Pharisees and the despised sinners is especially vivid in the stories of "the Pharisee and the tax collector" (Lk. 18:9-14) and of "the woman who was a great sinner" (Lk. 7:36-50).

Luke introduces the short moralizing story of the Pharisee and the tax collector with the words, "He also told this parable to some who trusted in themselves that they were righteous and despised others" (Lk. 18:9). The ensuing story then uses a Pharisee to illustrate this self-righteous, contemptuous behavior. Luke is far from intending to illustrate thereby the actual behavior of Pharisees in the Palestine of Jesus' time. Rather, he is contrasting the socially respectable (in the person of the Pharisee) and the socially despised (in the person of the tax collector). Those included in the "despised" are further specified as extortioners, lawbreakers (*adikoi*), and adulterers; the group is evidently a varied one. Alongside those whose activities are directly criminal (extortioners, lawbreakers) stand the tax collectors, whose very profession renders them suspect of illegal dealings, and others who are morally despicable (adulterers).

In the story of the dinner in the home of Simon the Pharisee the respected Pharisee is contrasted with a prostitute well known in the city. Here again no special emphasis is put on the fact that the host is a Pharisee. The emphasis is, rather, on the love Jesus shows for a notorious prostitute as a despised woman (*hamartōlos en tē polei*) ("a woman of the city, who was a sinner," Lk. 7:37), who is contemned by the respectable host, among others. Jesus does not by any means have a hostile attitude to his host. He uses an example from the world of business (the cancelation of debts) to show the man the meaning of his, Jesus', concern for the sinful woman (Lk. 7:41-43). In her own way the prostitute behaves appropriately toward Jesus by showing him the hospitality that the host neglected.

It is possible to give more concrete social definition to the group of despised "sinners" represented by the tax collector: they are ordinary people, tax collectors, prostitutes, extortioners, lawbreakers. It is more difficult to specify in like manner the group of socially respected people represented by the Pharisee. It may be said in general that not only do they regard themselves as respectable, but society in fact respects them. It is hardly possible, however, to locate them more precisely in sociological terms.

It can be said at least that they are prosperous folk, though not necessarily rich. They host dinners (Lk. 7:41; 14:1). Moreover, the incidents that take place at the meal in the house of a ruler who happened to be a Pharisee (14:1ff.) show that the behavior both of the host and of the guests is to be interpreted as socially abnormal. That is, Luke is not concerned to describe this behavior as religiously abnormal behavior resulting from hostility to Jesus. Thus the guests try to get the places of honor at table for themselves (14:7-11). The host is reproached for inviting only those of his own class (friends, rich neighbors, relatives) from whom he can expect an invitation in return (14:12-14).

We may make our point here by referring to another passage. The statement that "the scribes . . . love . . . the places of honor at feasts" (Lk. 20:46) sheds light, for the reader of Luke, on a characteristic form of social behavior, and not on the scribes as such. So too when the behavior of the scribes and Pharisees is not expressly presented as a manifestation of hostility to Jesus, it is to be taken as referring in Luke to the behavior of prosperous and respected Christians. The fact that these kinds of behavior are attributed to the scribes and Pharisees shows that they are seen from the outset as negative "manners."

Jesus, as Savior of the despised, is critically contrasted with the Pharisees (in particular). His special "liking for the dregs," which plays such a large part in Luke especially, is a concern for those whom society—respectable society—despises: ordinary people like lawbreakers. His solidarity with these people is in contrast with the refusal of respectable folk to associate with them. It is to these respectable folk that the behavior of Jesus is held up as an example. Like the elder brother in the parable of the lost son, they are urged to rejoice at the conversion of these sinners and to extend a welcoming hand to them.

It is clear by now that the concern of Jesus for despised sinners is not a concern for the economically poor. On the other hand, there is no mistaking the fact that, in Luke, Jesus is also concerned with those who are really poor. But this aspect of the social message of Jesus, which was at the center of the earliest tradition, is no longer central in the Gospel of Luke. It manifests itself in this Gospel in miraculous cures of the blind, the cripple, and the lepers (see, e.g., Lk. 4:31-37, 38-42; 5:12-16, 17-26; 6:6-11, 18f.). The fact that Luke too sees these sick people as poor is clear especially in the healing of a blind beggar (18:35-43). But it also emerges from the juxtapositions of the poor and the sick (4:18f.; 7:22; 14:13, 21).

The important point for Luke is that these people are the "objects" of Jesus' salvific activity. The fact that the blind see, the lame walk, and the deaf regain their hearing shows that, with the coming of Jesus, God's salvation has dawned. These miraculous cures are signs that the age of salvation has come. Luke expressly emphasizes the element of fulfillment by Jesus. In addition, he stresses the direct connection between the activity of Jesus and the corresponding prophetic anticipations. Thus when two disciples of John the Baptist come to Jesus and ask him, "Are you he who is to come, or shall we look for another?" they find him—only in Luke!—in the very act of performing these signs that salvation has come: "In that hour he cured many of diseases and plagues and evil spirits, and on many that were blind he bestowed sight" (7:21). And immediately before this incident he had even, by restoring life to the young man of Nain, fulfilled the prophecies about the raising of the dead (7:11-17; only in Luke).

Luke is thus profoundly interested in the fact that the coming of Jesus marks the beginning of the time of salvation. Nor is there any question but that even in Luke's eyes Jesus concerns himself especially with the poor when he cures the sick. Nonetheless, for Luke the meaning of "good news for the poor" is not exhausted by these signs of salvation. When Luke speaks of good news for the poor he is referring to the Beatitude of the poor disciples and understands this message as specifically a criticism of the rich.

In Jesus' "inaugural sermon" at Nazareth, Luke gives a programmatic statement of "the good news for the poor":

"The Spirit of the Lord is upon me,
because he has anointed me to preach good news to the poor.
He has sent me to proclaim release to the captives
and recovering of sight to the blind,
to set at liberty those who are oppressed,
to proclaim the acceptable year of the Lord."
And he closed the book, and gave it back to the attendant, and sat down;
and the eyes of all in the synagogue were fixed on him. And he began to
say to them, "Today this scripture has been fulfilled in your hearing"
[Lk. 4:18-21].

The same linking is to be found in Jesus' answer to the question put by the Baptist's disciples: " . . . the blind receive their sight, the lame walk, lepers are cleansed, and the deaf hear, the dead are raised up, the poor have good news preached to them" (Lk. 7:22).

The fulfillment of salvation through the presence of Jesus consists in the healing of the sick and the preaching of good news to the poor. These are signs that God is now exercising his kingly rule. But the poor to whom the good news is preached (*ptōchoi euangelizontai*) are in fact the disciples. This follows necessarily from the meaning of the word *ptōchos* ("poor") in Luke. This Gospel consistently defines the word in economic and social terms. Therefore Luke does not use it in a transferred sense (as meaning "devout," e.g.). Therefore, too, we cannot identify the good news for the poor with the concern Jesus shows for tax collectors and other sinners. Moreover, since the good news for the poor is understood as a sign of salvation and therefore of the *basileia* that is present in Jesus, this "program" of Jesus cannot be separated from the context of his earthly ministry. In summary, "poor" refers to the poor disciples of Jesus, who have become *ptōchoi* as a result of their complete renunciation of possessions.

The same conclusion follows from Luke's use of the word *euangelizesthai* ("preach the good news"). Luke uses this verb more frequently than any of the other evangelists, but, apart from the passages already cited (4:18 and 7:22), he uses it in a general sense of the preaching activity of Jesus or his disciples (see, e.g., 4:43; 8:1; 9:6; 16:16). Yet the only passage that can be interpreted as saying what the content of *ptōchoi euangelizontai* is, is the Beatitude of the poor disciples. In other words, only here do we have the substance of the proclamation of salvation to the poor. For here there is a specific pledge of participation in the kingdom of God *now,* and a pledge given to those who are poor in the economic sense, even though they voluntarily made themselves such. Moreover, since in Luke's view *euangelizesthai* ("preach the good news") is connected, during the earthly ministry of Jesus, with the idea of the *basileia tou Theou* ("kingdom [or reign] of God"), the Beatitude of the poor disciples is the closest thing to a pledge of their participation in the now present *basileia tou Theou.*

This interpretation is confirmed by the contrast between the Beatitude of the poor and the woes pronounced on the rich. The contrast shows that the kingdom of God is promised to the poor and not to the rich. Thus the Beatitude of the poor disciples proves to be in every way the fulfillment of the program according to which the good news is preached to the poor. The poor disciples are given a participation in the present *basileia*; thus they possess that which the *euangelizesthai* has for its content. At the same time they are called blessed because they are poor (*ptōchoi*), and thus they verify in themselves the second part of the sign of salvation. This gift of salvation is given to them, the poor, and not to the rich; once again the critique of the rich is unmistakable.

We have now seen that in Luke each of the two themes—Jesus as Savior of sinners, and the good news for the poor—has its critical message for the respected and wealthy. The rich are confronted with the message of salvation as intended specifically for the poor; the respected are faced with Jesus' concern for the despised. The rich and the respected of the present time, that is, in the community Luke has in view, must therefore feel that they are being addressed. Jesus, of course, is no longer on earth, and the life lived by the poor disciples of Jesus is also something of the past. But the rich and the respected still exist, and so do the people they look down upon.

In this sense Luke is the evangelist of the rich and the respected. His purpose is not to present the message and behavior of Jesus or his disciples in such a manner that the rich and respected can in conscience accept their own way of life. Rather, he wants the rich and respected to be reconciled to the message and way of life of Jesus and his disciples; he wants to motivate them to a conversion that is in keeping with the social message of Jesus. He pursues this goal by means of a critique of the rich and respected that in its scope and radicality is unmatched elsewhere in the New Testament. At the same time, however, he also makes use of a broad and demanding paraenesis to which we must return later on.

One final point can provide further confirmation of our thesis that Luke addresses his social message primarily to rich and respected Christians. Though he speaks so often of "good news for the poor," he knows much less about their lives than he does about the lives of the rich. He takes his description of the life of the poor from the earliest tradition (Lk. 1:53; 6:20f.; 16:20f.; 18:35), but does not further visualize it from the viewpoint of the poor themselves. He has a much better acquaintance with the life of the prosperous and the respected. This is shown in an especially vivid way by the topos of the banquet, which Luke uses so frequently.

2. The Transgressions of the Rich

The following texts in Luke's Gospel show him in critical confrontation with rich Christians: 1:53; 6:24–26; 8:14; 12:13ff.; 14:15ff.; 16:14f., 19–31; 21:34. In this connection some passages in Acts must also be taken into account: 1:18f.; 5:1–11; 8:18ff. For the moment we shall exclude from consideration those texts that give Luke's interpretation of the message about the eschatological reversal of social destinies as provided by the earliest Jesus tradition (Lk. 1:53; 6:24–26; 14:15–24; 16:19–31); these will be discussed together in the next section, "Woe to the Rich." At present we shall be concerned primarily with the transgressions of the rich as shown in their failures of faith (8:14) and as conceptualized in the vices of *philargyria* ("love of money, avarice," Lk. 16:14) and *pleonexia* ("greed, covetousness," Lk. 12:15).

LUKE 8:14

This verse is basic for understanding the experiences that preachers of the gospel have of rich Christians: "As for what fell among the thorns, they are those who hear [the word of God], but as they go on their way they are choked by the cares and riches and pleasures of life, and their fruit does not mature." The verse is part of the explanation of the well-known parable of the sower, which Luke has taken over, together with its allegorical interpretation, from his Marcan model (cf. Lk. 8:14–15 and Mk. 4:1–20). Luke, however, gives a sparer version of both parable and interpretation and makes not only stylistic changes in his model but also some notable alterations.

The information that Luke supplies about the audience already indicates a clear interest: among the crowd he numbers hearers from the cities (*kata polin*) that Jesus has previously visited (Lk. 8:4). Luke deliberately creates this particular audience so that he can address city-dwellers in the following fundamental parable about the reception of God's word. Verse 14 in particular presupposes an urban milieu. For this and other reasons there is no doubt that in this pericope Luke has in mind the Christians of his own day.

Luke alters not only details of v. 14 but the entire sentence structure. At the outset, that which fell among thorns is identified with a specific group of hearers of God's word (*akousantes*). These hearers are, however, the subject of the sentence in Luke, whereas in Mark all statements have the word for subject.

Consequently, in Luke it is not the word that is "choked," but the hearers of the word, and these are choked specifically in their way of life—their "going" (*poreuomenoi*)—and do not bring fruit to maturity. The "going on their way" refers to the hearers' life of faith, which of course includes their entire way of life (cf. Lk. 1:6; Acts 9:31; 14:16).

The hearers are choked by "cares" (*merimnai*), "riches" (*ploutos*), and the "pleasures of life" (*hēdonai tou biou*). A comparison with Mark shows that Luke excludes any possibility of relativizing these dangers. At the center of the list is that which is a special threat to the Christian life of faith, namely, riches. For Mark riches is but one problem among others and is in fact dangerous only in certain circumstances, namely, when the hearers succumb to the seduction of riches (*apatē tou ploutou*). For Luke, on the contrary, the very possession of riches is already dangerous for Christians. The cares and pleasures of life do not seem to be separate dangers that are juxtaposed to riches but, rather, threats that go together with riches. This is shown by Lk. 21:34, which can be taken as a commentary on Lk. 8:14: "But take heed to yourselves lest your hearts be weighed down with dissipation and drunkenness and cares about possessions, and that day come upon you suddenly" (authors' translation).

In 8:14, then, Luke emphasizes the point that cares, riches, and the pleasures of life choke the hearers as they live their lives, so that they do not bring any fruit to maturity (*telesphoreō*). Luke's metaphor of the growth of fruit must, of course, not be pressed too hard. It is notable, nonetheless, that whereas Mark speaks of the word not bringing forth any fruit at all in these hearers, Luke speaks of the hearers not bringing any fruit to maturity. He does not deny that this group has heard the word and that they have in principle adopted a way of life proper to those who have heard it. Their progress, however, is blocked by cares, riches, and the pleasures of life; they do not reach the goal. This goal is named in verse 15: *karpophorousin en hypomonē* ("bring forth fruit in patience").

Those who hear in the proper manner lead a life consistent with the word. The consistency is due to the fact that they hold the word fast "in an honest and good heart" (*en kardia lakē kai agathē*). The concept of *kalokagathia* ("nobility of heart") that lurks here beneath the surface of the words would already make a Hellenistic reader think of deeds produced by this way of life. The same idea is expressed in Lk. 6:45 in a saying from the Sayings-source: "The good man out of the good treasure of his heart produces good, and the evil man out of his evil treasure produces evil; for out of the abundance of the heart his mouth speaks." The person's heart determines his or her actions. The hearts of the rich are possessed by the pleasures of life and worries about possessions; therefore they do not bring to maturity the good deeds that are the fruit of the word. Prosperous Christians have heard the word of God but their active following of the word is hindered by cares, riches, and pleasures; they have heard, but they do not live consistently with what they have heard. They do no good works, bring forth no fruits worthy of their conversion (see Lk. 3:8).

They belong to the church but do not do what the word of the Lord bids them do (Lk. 6:46).

It is the failure of the rich that concerns Luke. The rich are contrasted not, as in Mark, with Christians who bear fruit thirty-, sixty-, or a hundredfold (Mk. 4:20), but with those who bear fruit in patience, that is, who bear it not just once but perseveringly (*en hypomonē*). *Hypomonē* ("patience") means, for Luke, steadfastness, persistence, endurance, and is to be understood here, as in Rom. 2:7, as perseverance in doing good. For that is precisely what is meant by the "fruit-bearing" of the good hearers with whom the rich are contrasted as poor hearers.

In reading Lk. 8:14, then, we must not think of a situation of persecution or the problem of the lengthy period before the Parousia. The endurance that is meant here is hindered by cares, riches, and the pleasures of life, and not by external influences such as persecution or the problem of the delayed Parousia. The interpretation of 8:14 that we have given is more appropriate to a Christian community at about the end of the first century. In such a community attention is focused not so much on threats from outside or on the problem of conversion to the faith. It is the living of the faith that creates problems, and these problems do not arise from the fact that Christ's coming has been delayed. The life of faith is threatened by tangible circumstances: riches, cares, and the pleasures of life.

PHILARGYRIA, OR LOVE OF MONEY, AVARICE

Our Christian tradition of biblical exegesis has accustomed us to think of warnings against debauchery, drunkenness, and in general the pleasures of life as priggish, "pious" efforts to restrict our keen enjoyment of life; we are therefore reserved toward New Testament exhortations in this area. But while we cannot completely deny that Luke is somewhat inclined to an "ascetic" view of life, we must also observe that his warnings have his critique of the rich for their context and that he uses in his exhortations familiar key words from the Hellenistic ethics of his day. The pleasures of life that he criticizes are the pleasures of the rich, not pleasures in the comprehensive sense in which they are forbidden by an ascetical moral code. Criticism of the rich is also indicated by the use of two concepts that have a fixed place in the ethical treatment of wealth: *philargyria* ("love of money, avarice") and *pleonexia* ("greed, covetousness").

Luke calls the Pharisees "lovers of money": "The Pharisees, who were lovers of money (*philargyroi*), heard all this, and they scoffed at him. But he said to them, 'You are those who justify yourselves before men, but God knows your hearts; for what is exalted among men is an abomination in the sight of God' " (16:14f.). *Philargyria* was a regular topic of philosophical instruction. We need only refer to Diogenes Laertius. In his *Lives* Diogenes the Cynic calls love of money "the mother-city of all evils." In Luke love of money is to be understood against the background of the story of the unjust steward and its application to Christians. In interpreting the passage we must bear in mind that

Jesus directs the story to the disciples (Lk. 16:1). Still presupposed at this point is the audience description of Lk. 15:1ff., according to which tax collectors and sinners, Pharisees and scribes, but also disciples (as 16:1 shows), have gathered around Jesus.

We must not mistakenly turn the warning against the service of mammon, which occurs in this context (Lk. 16:13), into a hermeneutical key to the entire passage. If we do, it will be impossible to explain why the disciples are being addressed here. They are voluntarily poor and the service of mammon can in general no longer be a problem for them. In point of fact, Luke is saying in 16:1-13 that the disciples can have legitimate money dealings; but then these dealings are no longer a service of mammon. These legitimate dealings consist in making friends by means of unrighteous mammon (v. 9) and thus handling the money of others (v. 12) in a conscientious way (vv. 10f.).

Though Luke does not explain what he means concretely by "making friends," the reference is doubtless to Christian caritative activity or what Luke elsewhere describes as "doing good." He is here making use of a topos in Hellenistic ethics,[30] even while transforming it in his characteristic way. The reward that will be given for "making friends" (an activity to be understood as "doing good") will not be received in the times of need that may come later on, but will be bestowed in heaven. Thus one uses transient mammon to win for oneself an imperishable treasure in heaven. The phrase "when it fails" (*hotan eklipē*, v. 9) is to be compared with the "treasure that does not fail" (*thēsauron anekleipton*) of 12:33.

The scoffing of the money-loving Pharisees at the instruction of Jesus renders our explanation probable, for their mockery is directed at his words insofar as they are open to misinterpretation, that is, insofar as they are open to the reproach of mammon-service. Luke is contrasting the disciples and their responsible handling of others' money with the Pharisees and their love of money. We need not prove once again that, in speaking of the Pharisees, Luke has rich and respectable Christians in mind as his contemporary addressees. The Pharisees are here again being described in terms of their love of money and their self-righteousness, not as religious opponents of Jesus. On the other hand, the offensive behavior of the steward who manipulates promissory notes is presented here as exemplary and prudent only insofar as he uses unrighteous mammon to create a claim for future favors from those whose debts he helps to cancel.

In dealing with their own generation the "sons of light" can learn from the prudence shown by the "sons of this world" in dealing with theirs. The sons of light are to act like the steward, but on an entirely different level. God knows their hearts and judges accordingly their handling of unrighteous mammon, whereas he sees "love of money" in the hearts of the Pharisees who think themselves righteous in this area. In *philous poiein* ("making friends"), the disciples do not gain any earthly advantage; their dealings with unrighteous mammon will bring only a heavenly reward ("that they may receive you into the heavenly habitations").

In this passage, unlike others discussed earlier in which the disciples are the addressees, it seems possible to apply directly to Luke's present community the instruction given to the disciples. He probably wants to tell his respected and prosperous Christians that a person's heart decides whether or not his or her handling of money is mammon-service, and therefore that love of money is not simply one trait among others but involves the whole moral identity of the person. That is what Luke has in mind when he speaks of the "heart." If, then, God sees love of money in the hearts of the Pharisees, we are not to think simply of their motives and intentions in handling money; the issue is, rather, the entire orientation of their lives. In the eyes of other human beings, who see only externals, this orientation may be noble. God, however, sees the heart, and what is noble to human beings is in this case an abomination to God.

The story of Ananias and Sapphira (Acts 5:1-11) also shows the important role played by the heart in money matters. These two individuals had sold a piece of property but had kept part of the proceeds for themselves and concealed this fact. They took this decision in their hearts. Satan had filled their hearts, and the lie they told was told to God, not to other human beings. Simon Magus, too, had an insincere heart. He committed a crime in his heart when he tried to buy the power to bestow the Spirit (Acts 8:9-25).

PLEONEXIA, OR GREED, COVETOUSNESS

Greed is closely related to love of money. It is a desire of ever more money; it is a sickness of the soul, which is unable to find rest. In his essay on "the passionate desire for riches," Plutarch describes greed as being, like love of money, an insatiable longing for wealth that brings tribulations, troubles, and sleepless nights. Greed drives out such virtues as compassion, kindness to friends, and level-headedness, and replaces them with flattery, ambition, and vanity. Elsewhere too in Hellenistic moral exhortation, greed is the vice of vices and one of the more important causes of evil in the world.[31] Chrysostom devotes an entire discourse to it (*Oratio* 67); he already expresses the view that it is God who punishes the greedy (6, 67).

In Hellenistic ethics *pleonexia* is described in such negative terms that a greater evil hardly seems possible. The concepts and categories used in defining it are derived at times from religion, at times from individual ethics, at times from social ethics: greed brings frustration; it is a transgression against the gods; it is also harmful to society. Greed can even be regarded as a spurious ideal that wrongly finds the meaning of life in the earning of money. Plutarch sums up the educational ideals of the greedy and the miserly: "You must concentrate on earning and saving. Never forget: your worth depends on what you have."[32] Jesus' warning against greed is directly contrary to the kind of wisdom that is based on love of money: "Take heed, and beware of all covetousness; for a man's life does not consist in the abundance of his possessions" (Lk. 12:15).

This warning against *pleonexia* is occasioned by a request from an anonymous man in the crowd who asks Jesus to act as judge and settle his dispute with his brother over an inheritance. Jesus curtly rejects the request: "Man, who made me a judge or divider over you?" (Lk. 12:14). The dispute over the inheritance arises out of greed, as is said in Lk. 12:15. The following story of the rich but foolish farmer (vv. 16–21) provides a specific illustration of greed or covetousness at work.

From an economic standpoint the rich farmer acts prudently: he stores up his record harvest and prepares (*hetoimazein*) for harder times. But since he is able to save his grain in this way and was already rich before his record harvest (he is in fact introduced as "a rich man"), we must not think that he builds his new barns as storage for his own consumption. Rather, he stores up the harvest in his great new barns against the harder times when he will be able to sell it at a far better price. His soliloquy, "Take your ease, eat, drink, be merry" (Lk. 12:19), does not reflect therefore the repose of a farmer who has at last harvested so much grain that he need not go hungry in the coming years. The rest that the rich farmer seeks is rest from the constant earning of money. Now, after this record harvest, he is able (he thinks) and certainly wants to take his ease, enjoy his possessions, and live off the fruits of his restless industry. But he has another think coming. In storing up grain in his great new barns, he has taken part in an economic crime that is of major importance in the economy of antiquity. He has not simply secured his own future in a relatively harmless way; he has harmed society by holding back his harvests. That is what drives up the price of grain.[33]

The self-enjoyment of the rich man is thus first and foremost behavior that is harmful to society and consists in a brazen accumulation of grain or other agricultural products for the purpose of ensuring a higher profit margin. The death of the speculator occurs at the very moment when he thinks he is at last able to desist from his restless quest of profit and enjoy a carefree life. The concluding saying gives a negative interpretation of his behavior as a whole: "So is he who lays up treasure for himself, and is not rich before God" (Lk. 12:21). There is no middle course between "laying up treasure" and "being rich before God."

Were it not for the introduction (vv. 13–15) and the conclusion (v. 21), this story might be thought of as told by poor folk to illustrate the just deserts of a "hoarder." Only with difficulty, on the other hand, could it be put in the mouths of the rich as an exhortation to the timely enjoyment of one's possessions; only verse 20 would serve this purpose. In its context in Luke the story clearly becomes a stringent critique of the greedy man whose whole life is out of tune because he sees his life as getting its meaning from abundant possessions (v. 15). The orientation that life ought to have is described in the phrase *eis theon plouton* ("being rich before God"). "Rich before God" sums up for Luke all the positive ethical actions a rich Christian must perform.[34] Of this we shall speak later.

In conclusion we must refer once again to the fundamental meaning of the contrast between the covetousness of the rich farmer and the voluntary poverty of the disciples. This contrast dominates Luke 12. Thus immediately after the story of the grain speculator, Luke puts an address of Jesus to his disciples: "And he said to his disciples, 'Therefore I tell you, do not be anxious about your life, what you shall eat, nor about your body, what you shall put on' " (12:22). Luke is here drawing a conclusion for the disciples from the story of the rich farmer. He takes the opening *dia touto* ("therefore") from the Sayings-source (cf. Mt. 6:25), but he places it in a new context. He applies the words "do not be anxious" directly to the disciples and contrasts this lack of anxiety with the greedy precautions of the rich man.

The lifestyle of the disciples and the demands Jesus makes of them are in glaring contradiction to the rich man and his behavior. Here we see the basic meaning that the voluntary poverty of the disciples has even for the time of Luke. But the question asked by rich Christians, "What are we to do?" is not yet fully answered by pointing to the lifestyle of the disciples of Jesus. The reason for saying this is that the demands made of the disciples are not made of the Christians of Luke's day in the same *measure*. The voluntary poverty of the disciples does, however, indicate the direction in principle, and Luke asks not a little of the Christians of his own day.

The question we ask today, namely, how the readers of the Gospel in Luke's time could understand these distinctions, is doubtless born of the situation in exegesis, where practically all texts in the Gospel are located theoretically on the same level. But such a question does not arise in the concrete situation of a community of Christians (such as Luke's community) whose problems are colored by the coexistence of richer and poorer, respected and despised members. These Christians know Jesus is no longer with them but is in heaven. They realize that the following of Jesus consists therefore not in a simple slavish imitation, a reproduction of the past, but rather, in its "repetition" in the conditions of the present time.

So too those living today in a concrete Christian community do not think, any more than Luke's Christians did, of interpreting the demands made by Jesus of his disciples as demands made directly of them or their community. At the same time, however, they experience not only the temporal distance between themselves and the disciples but also a material distance. That is, they experience the lifestyle of the disciples as a critical challenge to their own lifestyle and that of their community. All the more urgently therefore they ask themselves the question, "What shall we do?" In this situation they can apply Luke's positive ethics directly to themselves, especially if theirs is a prosperous community. Even without instruction in exegesis they recognize that Luke has them or their community in mind. Exegetes will probably always have to labor making distinctions that are immediately evident in the vital situation of a Christian community.

3. Woe to the Rich

The contrast between the story of the covetous rich man and the address of Jesus to his disciples on deceptive and legitimate "anxieties" contains a suggestion of a theme that Luke develops explicitly in other contexts: the theme of the reversal of (social) destinies. He derives the theme from the earliest Jesus tradition. He has, therefore, a serious interest in the problem. In the passage we have just been discussing the theme or problem suggests itself in this way: the rich man who made covetous provision for his prosperous life dies, while the disciples, whose first concern is for the kingdom of God, receive food, drink, and clothing as well.

The theme of the eschatological reversal of social destinies already emerges with full clarity in the Magnificat of Mary: "He [God] has shown strength with this arm,/he has scattered the proud in the imagination of their hearts,/he has put down the mighty from their thrones,/and exalted those low degree;/he has filled the hungry with good things,/and the rich he has sent empty away" (Lk. 1:51-53). The theme is then more fully developed in the Sermon on the Plain (6:20-26), though here it takes pointed form in the contrast between the poor disciples and the rich. The same motif controls the story of the rich spendthrift and poor Lazarus; it becomes explicit there in 16:25: "Abraham said, 'Son, remember that you in your lifetime received your good things, and Lazarus in like manner evil things; but now he is comforted here, and you are in anguish."

Regardless of whether or not Luke found the woe-sayings on the rich in the Sayings-source, there is no doubt that he took the motif of the eschatological reversal of social destinies from existing Christian tradition. But did he understand it in the same way as the poor disciples of Jesus had? Our purpose at this point is to understand the function of this eschatological reversal in Luke and in the context created by the sociohistorical structures of his day.

As a help in understanding Luke's interest in the problem, let us begin by considering the results thus far gained and reflecting on the fact that Luke's social message is addressed to rich and respected Christians. The passages in Luke that speak of a reversal of social destinies are therefore located in a social and literary context that relates them to his critique of the prosperous and to the rules of behavior that this critique proposes. Consequently, it is no longer possible to understand the reversal motif as it had been understood in the earliest tradition. It must, rather, be interpreted as an admonition or warning to prosperous Christians. Is it possible to verify in the texts themselves such a shift in the intention governing the use of the motif? To answer this question we shall have to focus our interpretation on a text that undoubtedly displays Lucan authorship. We turn therefore to the story of the great banquet (14:15-24).

LUKE'S VERSION OF THE GREAT BANQUET

Jesus comes to dine in the home of a ruler who is a Pharisee (Lk. 14:1). After healing a dropsical man on the sabbath (14:2-6) and thereby challenging the lawyers and Pharisees, he addresses the invited guests in a parable about a banquet. Entirely in the style of Hellenistic paraenesis, in which behavior at a banquet could serve as a metaphor for behavior in life generally, he warns the guests: "Every one who exalts himself will be humbled, and he who humbles himself will be exalted" (v. 11).

In this parable Jesus is addressing men who set great store on social recognition. The term *prōtoklisia* ("place of honor") is here used metaphorically of any recognition by society and does not refer solely to places at table (v. 7). Jesus is therefore warning people who are bent on getting to the top socially that in God's future they will experience a reversal and find themselves at the bottom.

He then turns to the host, the ruler who is a Pharisee, and exhorts him directly, without recourse to a parable: the host should not follow the principle of tit for tat and invite those who will invite him in turn (relatives, friends, rich neighbors). Rather, he should invite the poor, the crippled, the blind, the lame, that is, people who certainly cannot repay this good deed. He will then have his reward in God's future (Lk. 14:12–14). Jesus' ethical admonitions thus have an eschatological aspect. The host will even be *makarios* ("blessed") if he follows the advice of Jesus.

This Beatitude inevitably provokes opposition. It is expressed by one of the guests, who thereby elicits from Jesus the parable of the great banquet. "When one of those who sat at table with him heard this, he said to him, 'Blessed is he who shall eat bread in the kingdom of God!' " (v. 15). The context makes it clear that the man's remark is intended as a contradiction and not simply as a neutral continuation of the theme. For the answer Jesus gives presupposes that the other guest's intervention is critical of his earlier macarism. The man's objection can probably be put this way: it is not yet settled that they who invite the poor and other beggars to table will be rewarded at the resurrection of the just; let us therefore say that they are to be called blessed who will in fact share in the banquet in the kingdom of God. The man does not say who "they" are, but there could be no doubt in the minds of the self-righteous "scribes" and "Pharisees": they themselves would be the ones to sit at table in the kingdom.

It is to this implicit claim that the parable of the great banquet responds. It would be a mistake, however, to interpret the opposition between the other guests and Jesus as religious: Jews (Israel) vs. pagans (Christians). The entire context shows that the focus of attention is on socially defined patterns of action or oppositions, as the case may be. There is an explicit contrast between friends, relatives, and rich neighbors, on the one side, and the poor and crippled, on the other (v. 12). The same collection of poor folk reappears in verse 21. Nor is there any reason for saying that the reference is, for example, to tax collectors and sinners. If that was what Luke meant, he would probably have come out and said so.[35] But let us look now at Jesus' answer to the objection raised by his fellow guest.

A prosperous man sends invitations to a banquet. When his servant asks those invited to come to table, they excuse themselves one after another. One has just bought five yoke of oxen, another has just bought a field, another has just married. The host is angered and has his servant go into the streets and lanes of the city and bring in the poor, crippled, blind, and lame for the banquet. But there are still empty places. He therefore sends his servant out again, this time to bring guests in from outside the city. The parable of the banquet ends with the saying: "For I tell you, none of those men who were invited shall taste my banquet" (v. 24).

The parable is meant to illustrate God's call to the heavenly banquet. Its meaning, however, can be grasped only if we understand the level of concrete reality on which the story moves. The man (*anthropos tis*) who gives the banquet must be pictured as very prosperous and respected. This is clear not only from the fact that in the final analysis his behavior symbolizes that of God. The kind of guests who have been invited also tells us that the host occupies a high position in society. One of the guests excuses himself because he has bought five yoke of oxen, that is, ten draft animals; then such animals could plow about 45 hectares of land. Since the man is probably not buying such animals for the first time, he doubtless has a large estate.[36] Moreover, the scene of the story is the city, a fact that is not inconsistent with two of the guests giving excuses referring to agriculture. On the contrary, this is all the more evidence that these guests are prosperous landowners who are able to live in the city. By any accounting, the story is set in a prosperous milieu.

A comparison with the parallel story in Matthew (22:1–14) shows, among other things, that Luke is especially interested in the excuses offered and in the social rank of the "substitute guests." The excuses are meant seriously and are not farfetched; they reflect in a realistic way the social position of the invited guests. It is true, of course, that the excuses can appear foolish only when compared with the invitation. One cannot sympathize with the attitude of the invited guests unless one fails to take into account the supposition behind the parable, namely, that there are no reasonable excuses for refusing to come. Only this supposition renders intelligible the anger of the *kyrios* or *oikodespotēs* ("master" or "householder") at the disregard of his invitation.

A contemporary reader would react in the same way to the behavior of the invited guests. A prudent man looking to his own advantage would not refuse the invitation of such a high-ranking person. On the contrary, he would want it and would try to attend this kind of dinner, even if he were not officially invited. We must bear in mind the importance of such receptions in the Roman imperial period; they provided opportunities for improving one's social standing and economic position. When Pliny, for example, had to refuse a dinner invitation from Valerius Paulinus, he excused himself in the most obsequious way: unfortunately he had to attend without delay to the leasing of his farms.[37] In such a milieu even a rich man had to excuse himself for nonattendance upon a man of still higher standing. At this period and in these circles no one could have offered a new marriage as an excuse and not have thereby ruined himself socially and made himself a laughingstock.[38] In the eyes of those who knew the value of such an invitation, the excuses offered in the parable must have amounted to a foolish disregard of the host. One did not lose that kind of opportunity for social recognition and resultant economic advantage. One would have to be under the urgent necessity of leasing all his estates and, in addition, be weary of the competition for the favor of the more powerful (as Pliny was), before rejecting such an invitation.

That background also helps us to assess the excuses when the invitation in question is an invitation to the eschatological banquet. Prosperous Christians behave just as foolishly as the invited guests in the parable. They regard acquisition of a property or the purchase of draft animals—in short, their business dealings—as more important than the invitation they have received to God's banquet. The banquet is ready, but they give preference to their objectively less important business and disregard the Lord's invitation. The parable explains their folly to them in terms they can understand and appreciate: they would not behave the same way if invited by one more powerful than they. Even the man who excuses himself because he has just married would not offer such an excuse; rather, he would postpone his wedding. Yet when invited to the heavenly banquet he does not choose postponement. When invited into the *basileia* the prosperous cannot bring themselves to regard their own business as less important than the invitation.

These prosperous Christians have foolishly rejected the invitation for the sake of business or a marriage; therefore they will not taste of the banquet in the kingdom. Their places will be taken by the poorest of the poor—both the poor of the city, whose illnesses prevent them from moving away,[39] and the poor with no fixed abode, who stay outside the city and must be compelled to accept the invitation. The reversal of the original seating plan is utterly complete. All the destitute within reach will replace the prosperous folk at the festivities in the kingdom of God. Those originally invited will not taste of the banquet in God's kingdom.

This reversal of destinies in the future kingdom of God is not accompanied by any description of future suffering that would serve to balance out present prosperity or of future prosperity to balance out present distress. Luke is concerned, rather, to show that the businessmen and the man just married are losing their participation in the heavenly banquet by their present behavior as such. Their place is taken by the poor and the sick or, in a word, by beggars. The replacement of those first invited by others is indeed motivated by the idea of retribution, but the goal of the replacement is not a balancing out of earthly social destinies, of the kind of life previously experienced (the poor are consoled, the rich suffer). The intention is to warn and exhort the businessmen and the man just married. Their replacement by beggars is meant to serve this purpose. The beggars are not invited to enjoy the meal for their own sakes but because those originally invited have forfeited the banquet by their behavior.

The story is thus not concerned with a strict reversal of the social destinies of rich and poor. The story does not console the poor; it does warn the rich. It is not the product of a starving man's imagination; the poorest of the poor would hardly think of themselves as eschatological "understudies." Again, the story hardly gives joy to the poor, but it does make the rich anxious. Their behavior in making business the important thing in their lives brings upon them the threat of eschatological retribution, that is, the withdrawal of the original invitation to the kingdom of God. Moreover, the story is told not in order that the rich may remain as they are, but in order that they may change.

In addition, the story does not announce a reversal of the present lot of the rich, that is, a loss of their wealth. For this reason it can easily be misunderstood. It can, for example, be interpreted as meaning that the poor are told to wait for their consolation and are meanwhile exploited as eschatological "understudies," while the rich are threatened with retribution on never-never day. Such an interpretation would overlook the fact that Luke is not a "social romantic" who threatens hard-boiled businessmen with exclusion from a party that their calculating minds tell them will never take place. Rather, he is addressing prosperous Christians who know they have received an invitation to the banquet and who regard it as important (see v. 15). They still set store by that entrance ticket.

Nor does Luke think it possible for the prosperous to receive a further special invitation. This is clear from the ending of the story about the rich man and poor Lazarus. There the rich man who is roasting in Hades and cannot change his own painful destiny appeals to Abraham:

> "Then I beg you, father, to send him [Lazarus] to my father's house, for I have five brothers, so that he may warn them, lest they also come into this place of torment." But Abraham said, "They have Moses and the prophets; let them hear them." And he said, "No, father Abraham; but if some one goes to them from the dead, they will repent." He said to him, "If they do not hear Moses and the prophets, neither will they be convinced if some one should rise from the dead" [Lk. 16:27–31].

Luke has in mind here a return of Lazarus from the dead in order to warn the wealthy brothers and tell them of the torments that await the rich in Hades. Lucian has a similar notion in his *Dialogues of the Dead.* [40] The content of the passage, which we summarize below, makes it helpful in discussing the ideas found in Luke.

In a short dialogue Diogenes the Cynic commissions Pollux (whose "turn for resurrection" comes tomorrow, Lucian remarks ironically) to bring a message to Menippus, another Cynic, in the upper world. Menippus does not know whether to laugh or cry at the world's bustle and folly (because is "anyone at all . . . quite sure about what follows death?"). Pollux is to say to Menippus: "Diogenes bids you, Menippus . . . . come down here [to the world of the dead], if you want much more to laugh at." In the underworld he will never stop laughing—"particularly when you see rich men, satraps and tyrants so humble and insignificant, with nothing to distinguish them but their groans, and see them weak and contemptible when they recall their life above." Diogenes bids Pollux deliver this message to the rich: "Why do you guard your gold, you senseless fools? Why do you punish yourselves, counting interest, and piling up talents on talents, when you must come down here shortly with no more than a penny?" As for the poor: "Tell the poor, my Spartan friend, who are many, displeased with life and pitying themselves for their poverty, not to cry and moan; describe to them our equality here, telling them how they'll see the rich of earth no better off there than they are themselves."[41]

Lucian cynically puts this parody of Cynic "moral" discourse in the mouth of the greatest of the Cynics; he intends thereby to strike a blow at his favorite enemies by having them voice his own mockery of the gods of the upper and lower worlds. But even though Lucian himself regards as fairy tales the idea of a return from the lower world and the stories told of relationships there, his very parody shows the climate of opinion in which Luke is to be understood. Luke is, of course, worlds apart from the skeptical and cynical Lucian. This shows not only in the fact that he can without irony tell such miraculous and legendary stories (in addition to the story of Dives and Lazarus, see the imposing miracle legends in Acts, e.g., 9:36ff. and 20:7ff.). Luke differs from Lucian also, and above all, in his seriousness and in his criticism of the rich or his positive advice to them, as the case may be. Luke could not possibly make his own Lucian's cynical words of consolation for the poor in the upper world. He does not imagine a simple equality of rich and poor in the lower world, but expects retribution for the rich after their deaths.

Luke thus still believes what Lucian regards as horror stories intended to frighten the rich. It is not Luke's lack of an "enlightened education," however, but his socioethical program that distinguishes him most from Lucian. The prosperous and enlightened contemporary for whom Lucian writes would therefore hardly be impressed by Luke's Gospel. Luke is not writing for that kind of person.

Lucian's nihilistic viewpoint emerges clearly in another passage of the *Dialogues of the Dead*. There Hermes tells Charon, the ferryman of the dead, about the hustle and bustle of the upper world, the ambition, the competition for offices, honors, and possessions. Why should it be so when all must soon meet Charon with a penny in their mouths? Charon wants to tell these people that they should spare themselves all their useless efforts. Hermes advises against it: they would simply stop their ears, whereas those who know the real situation need no advice or warning. The idea of social distinctions on earth makes its appearance here. When Charon sees what torments (death, sickness, suffering) must be endured even by the rich and by princes (all the people regarded as blissfully happy), he says: "But if even the favored few lead such tormented lives, we can imagine the lot of ordinary mortals (*idiōtai*)!"

Thus Lucian too regards any warning to the living as futile. Certainly there is no question for him of warning them against continuing to live their lives heedless of the poor. Rather, in view of death and the suffering in the world, these people should realize how vain their striving is. This is more in keeping with the viewpoint of one who has a "nihilistic" vision of the world.

Even though the social milieus presupposed by Luke and Lucian are comparable and the two writers make use of similar literary and mythological motifs, the contrast with Lucian's "nihilism" helps us to understand Luke better. It is not nihilistic resignation that makes Luke regard a warning to the rich by someone returned from the dead as futile, but rather, his experience of the rich. If the law and the prophets have not already moved them to repentance, a dead man returning will not be any more successful.

The rich know full well what their duty is. They simply have not in fact repented. That is precisely what Luke is talking to them about. The story of the rich man and poor Lazarus and the parable of the great banquet are told to them in order that they may reflect and be converted. If they fail to do so, they will experience what is said in the texts about the reversal of destinies. Luke agrees fully with the severity of these texts, which he has taken over from the earliest tradition. He makes use of it, however, to warn the rich as a social class about their future destiny if they simply remain rich and do not comply with the demand already made in the law and the prophets: the demand that they give alms, that is, deal charitably with the poor and the needy and thereby become rich before God. There is positive retribution, or reward, in the future kingdom of God for charitable activity in this world; the alternative is negative retribution there. It is to keep the prosperous and the rich from such a negative end that Luke criticizes them so extensively and calls them to repentance.

In fact, the rich even become "afraid." This is clear from a little episode in the Acts of the Apostles. In this scene Paul had an opportunity to defend his cause before Felix the Procurator. But when he "argued about justice and self-control and future judgment, Felix was alarmed and said, 'Go away for the present; when I have an opportunity I will summon you.' At the same time he hoped that money would be given him by Paul. So he sent for him often and conversed with him" (Acts 24:25f.). This corrupt governor became fearful when told of the future judgment. Great "fear" also came upon the whole community and on everyone who heard that Ananias and Sapphira had paid with their lives for trying to deceive God over money (Acts 5:11). This motif of fear may strike us as strange, but Luke evidently takes it very seriously (see also Lk. 12:4f. and Acts 8:24). Yet even this motif has for its purpose to move the Christians in question to repentance. What are they to do?

V. HOW CAN PROSPEROUS CHRISTIANS BE SAVED?

We must turn now to the question of how rich and respected Christians can be saved. We have been supposing all along that Luke does not exhaust what he has to say in criticism of the rich and respected. We expect him to have a positive ethical program for these people, since he is interested in their conversion and not in their definitive loss. The call to conversion is characteristic of this Gospel. No other Gospel has so much to say about Jesus' mission to call sinners to repentance. Luke expects this repentance and conversion not only of—"sinners"—in the narrow sense but also of those who despise "sinners."

Luke uses the concept *hamartōlos* ("sinner") with several extensions. In Lk. 19:7 and 7:37, 39, socially respected people apply the term *hamartōlos* to their socially despised fellows: in this case, a chief tax collector and a prostitute well known in the city. Luke himself also uses *hamartōlos* in referring to social outcasts (15:1f.). And even though the tax collector's confession of sinfulness (18:13) refers to his relation to God, the term also includes the self-accusation of a man who has transgressed. Luke has no doubt that tax collectors, prostitutes, and criminals (who were rightly outcasts) were to be found in the company of Jesus. His story of the "thieves on the cross" further depicts Jesus' encounter with criminals (23:39–43).

But these despised folk and criminals serve Luke as an example of something more fundamental, namely, of the conversion (*metanoia*) that all human beings need in relation to God. It is not only tax collectors and criminals who must say, "I am guilty before God." In the final analysis even the "Pharisees" who despise "sinners" must say, "God, be merciful to me a sinner," and must understand that part of their offense is precisely the fact that they despise sinners.

For Luke the transgressions from which human beings must desist are of course sins in God's eyes. But they are also concretely verifiable in the interhuman sphere: arrogance, self-righteousness, extortion, robbery, wastefulness. Therefore the concept "sinner" takes a socially concrete form in Luke. It serves as the basis on which he develops his soteriological program. In Lk. 15:1f. the word "sinner" has as it were both of the extensions (the social and theological) that we have just distinguished. Compare the confession of the lost son in the parable: "Father, I have sinned against heaven and before you" (Lk. 15:21). Again, Peter confesses himself a sinner in the presence of the Lord who has manifested himself (Lk. 5:8).

We must not play off against one another, or isolate from one another, the concrete social manifestation of sin and its theological aspect. In Luke's eyes each of these is permeable to the other. For him social oppositions such as are expressed in the contempt of the Pharisees for tax collectors play a part. So do economic distinctions—the gulf between rich and needy is not necessarily identical with that between respected and despised Christians. There can also be rich men who are despised (Zacchaeus); on the other hand, the money-loving Pharisees are among those who despise sinners.

What then does Luke look for from prosperous Christians? What "fruits that befit repentance" are they to produce? The following passages in particular are to be understood as instructions given (especially) to rich and respected Christians regarding the way they should act: Lk. 19:1–10; 3:10–14; various statements on almsgiving; Acts 20:33–35; and, above all (even if the choice seems surprising) the Lucan version of Jesus' command of love for enemies (Lk. 6:27–49).

1. Renunciation of Half One's Property (Lk. 19:1–10; 3:10–14).

In the story of the exemplary behavior of the rich chief tax collector named Zacchaeus (Lk. 19:1–10) there is a direct connection with the social group consisting of the rich. Zacchaeus is introduced as a chief tax collector (*architelōnēs*) and a rich man (*plousios*) (Lk. 19:2). At the same time, however, he is also a "sinner" (Lk. 19:7). We thus have an instance of a rich man who as a sinner is sought and found by Jesus. The characterization of Zacchaeus as a "sinner" corresponds fully to Luke's use of the term.

In Luke the turning of Jesus to sinners and their conversion go together. Moreover, he thinks of their conversion as taking no less concrete a form than their preceding transgression had taken. Consequently, the now converted Zacchaeus makes up for his transgression, insofar as this had been a violation of the law. He will pay back fourfold whatever he has gained through fraud (Lk. 19:8). In so doing, he accepts for himself the punishment prescribed in Roman law for theft. In addition, however, he will now give half of his goods to the poor (Lk. 19:8).

In Luke's intention this story of the rich chief tax collector has application at two levels. On the one hand, it is an example of the conversion of a person who is a sinner before God, a conversion of which every human being stands in need. On the other hand, it is concretely the conversion of a rich person and therefore a hint to rich Christians how they should conduct themselves. It is to be noted that Jesus does not call upon the rich tax collector to follow him. The man's behavior thus doubtless becomes a paradigm of what Luke expects from wealthy Christians.

Why does the chief tax collector renounce precisely half of his goods? Comparison with the full renunciation of the disciples may certainly play a role here, but this does not suffice to explain the rich man's renunciation of half of his wealth. There are, however, two other motifs that can explain Luke's call for a renunciation of half of one's possessions. The principal motif is the concrete social utopia envisaged by Luke, who wants property to be distributed equally among the prosperous and the needy Christians of the community; this is suggested by the idea of a man renouncing half of his possessions. We shall come back to this point later on.

The other motif, to which we turn now, is the model from which Luke derives the demand he makes of the rich. That model is the instruction given by the Baptist in his sermon on states of life (Lk. 3:10–14): "He who has two coats [tunics or undergarments], let him share with him who has none; and he who has food, let him do likewise" (3:11). An interpretation of this instruction in various contexts will yield three levels of statement. At the pre-Lucan level the instruction refers concretely to the solidarity of the poorest of the poor with one another. In Luke's interpretation it is understood as an instruction regarding the caritative activity of ordinary people. At the same time, however, it becomes a model for the measure of caritative activity that Luke expects from rich Christians.

Verse 11 of the Baptist's sermon on states of life is pre-Lucan, for it presupposes the social situation of the Palestinian poor, who must have felt happy if they had two undergarments (*chitōn*). In the spirit of Is. 58:7 (share your bread with the hungry, clothe the naked) the poorest of the poor are called to solidarity with one another. There is no question here of the prosperous being symbolically summoned to caritative action. The passage is to be taken literally: if one of these poor people in fact has two tunics (a clean one for the sabbath, another for everyday use), he should give one of them to someone else who has none. Similarly, if someone has food that can be stretched to feed two, he should share it with someone else who is hungry. The social situation presupposed here precludes the possibility of a Lucan redaction; Luke, we recall, talks rather cavalierly of possessing *himatia* ("mantles").

On literary and sociohistorical grounds the other two instructions in the sermon on states of life—those addressed to tax collectors and soldiers—must be ascribed to the work of the Lucan redactor. This fact necessarily conditions our understanding of the meaning of verse 11 in Luke 3.

"Tax collectors also came to be baptized, and said to him, 'Teacher, what shall we do?' And he said to them, 'Collect no more than is appointed you.' Soldiers also asked him, 'And we, what shall we do?' And he said to them, 'Rob no one by violence or by false accusation, and be content with your wages' " (Lk. 3:12-14). Some literary peculiarities in this passage point to a Lucan redaction. It is remarkable, for example, that only at this point in the Gospel tradition certain terms occur, which otherwise only Paul uses: *strateuomenoi* ("soldiers") and *opsōnion* ("wages"). Luke's hand shows especially when, in introducing the tax collectors' question, he refers to their desire for baptism. The introduction to the preceding sermon of John on penance likewise mentions the desire for baptism, this time with reference to the crowd (Lk. 3:7). Luke evidently regards it as important to bring out the fact that tax collectors ask for baptism. For later on again he—and he alone—notes that tax collectors had been baptized by John (Mt. 21:32 does not mention this).

Finally, for sociohistorical reasons the demands made of the tax collectors and soldiers do not fit in with the preceding sermon on penance and with verse 11 that concludes it. The earliest Jesus tradition tells indeed of the solidarity of Jesus or his disciples with the tax collectors (nothing is said there, however, of soldiers). But in that tradition we do not find the tax collectors being summoned to do penance. The poor followers of Jesus, who had but a minimum of food and clothing, would hardly have had any contacts with tax collectors since they would not be liable to market duties, or any other taxes for that matter. And it is hardly to be expected that these same poor people would have been violently robbed by soldiers. These two groups of ordinary people—tax collectors and soldiers—are much more likely to have played a part in concrete experiences of Luke himself or members of his community. On the other hand, the fact that verses 12-14 are connected with the situation created by John's preaching argues against an independent tradition. It is therefore very likely that the verses belong to the Lucan redaction.

It follows, then, that in Luke's interpretation of it, the Baptist's sermon on states of life is to be regarded as moral instruction for ordinary folk. The latter are exhorted to solidarity among themselves. More important than this for Luke is the concrete demand that tax collectors and soldiers cease their illegal behavior. Conversion for ordinary tax collectors and soldiers means, therefore, a turning away from their illegal schemes. That is precisely what even the rich chief tax collector does. The difference between him and the ordinary tax collector is that according to the provisions of the law he must repay fourfold whatever he has extorted. Thus the caritative activity of ordinary people takes the concrete form of solidarity and a readiness to help others even needier than themselves. In comparison with the "people" who are to compensate for what they lack through solidarity, caritative activity on the part of the rich takes arithmetical form: they are to give up half of their possessions.

Luke thus distinguishes between the various concrete results that are to "befit repentance," depending on the social "capacity" of the sinner who is called to repentance. The idea latent here—that each person is to do what he or she can—is found elsewhere in Luke. As he tells us in Acts, the Christians of Antioch decided that each of them according to his or her means should contribute to the support of the brethren in Judea who were threatened with famine (Acts 11:27-30). The manner in which Luke deals here with a call for compassion that originally referred to the poor of Palestine throws light on his whole social gospel. He applies the original intention behind solidarity in distress to the concrete situation of his own community and links it to his concern for the conversion of sinners.

The turning away from illegal activity or, as the case may be, the expected caritative activity that conversion entails is thus measured by the social status of each person. Luke does not therefore offer an ethic of undifferentiated "almsgiving"; rather, he develops a properly social ethic, which has for its main focus Christians who enjoy prosperity. The term "alms" can suggest the mistaken notion that there is question here only of small donations, which do not hurt the giver and relieve at least the extreme distress of the recipient. In fact, however, Luke has a far more comprehensive idea of "almsgiving."

2. Charity to the Poor (Almsgiving)

Apart from Mt. 6:1-4 the term eleēmosynē ("alms") occurs in the New Testament only in the Gospel of Luke and in Acts (Lk. 11:41; 12:33; Acts 3:2, 3, 10; 9:36; 10:24, 31; 24:17). This statistic already makes it clear that Luke considers important the reality designated by the word "alms." His first concern, therefore, is to impress upon the minds of his community that caritative works of mercy are part of Christian life. To a community made up of Hellenistic Christians, this truth is by no means a self-evident one. A comparison with Mt. 6:1-4 shows that the latter is no doubt able to presuppose in his community the usual Jewish practice of almsgiving. This is not the case for Luke. Moreover, care of the poor in the Jewish synagogues and in Matthew is caritative activity directed primarily to coreligionists. In Luke, on the other hand, "alms" refers to charity directed to non-Christians.

When Luke uses the term "alms," he has in mind first and foremost those who are its recipients, namely, destitute persons. This viewpoint emerges with special vividness in the story of the healing of a man who has been lame since birth (Acts 3:1-11). The cripple begs alms from passersby. The connection between "alms" and the destitute poor also becomes clear from the fact that two demands made of the disciples are interchangeable: to sell one's goods and give the proceeds as alms (Lk. 12:33) and to sell one's goods and distribute the proceeds to the poor (Lk. 18:22).

Alms need not, however, take the form of money; they can also take the form of good works (see Acts 9:36). As a matter of fact, Luke has no special interest in determining the form alms are to take. His concern is that alms be given or, as the case may be, that Christians understand almsgiving to be an exercise of Christian piety and a necessary element in a life inspired by faith (see Lk. 11:39-41 and Acts 10:1ff.). Neither the advice to the Pharisees, "Give for alms those things which are within; and behold, everything is clean for you" (Lk. 11:41), nor the description of Cornelius, the exemplary devout centurion, tells us what "alms" means concretely.

Luke can give the concept *eleēmosynē* ("alms") a wide variety of applications. It can include both a small gift to a beggar and the liberal charity of Cornelius, the centurion (Acts 10:2). One may be asked to give all he has as alms; on the other hand, almsgiving may simply be urged in a general way as an exercise of piety. Given the variability in the referent of the concept, we will be well advised to understand it in a general way as charity or caritative activity. On the other hand, one restriction is called for. Jesus son of Sirach has an even more comprehensive conception of alms, but it applies only to equals: "It is not right to do good to the man who persists in evil or to him who does not give charity (*eleēmosynē*) in return" (Sir. 12:3; authors' translation). Luke does not use the term in the sense of good deeds among equals, for which a return is expected. On the contrary, in his use of the word, "almsgiving" is the duty of Christians to be compassionate to the poorest of the poor.

Luke does not seem to know of any organized care of the poor such as was practiced among the Jews or in later Christian communities. At most, traces of such organization may be seen in the story of Tabitha, a disciple who made clothing for the poor. The scantiness of information on any organized care of the poor may be due to the fact that Luke is thinking of poor non-Christians and that in such cases there was no organized care by the community as such but the matter was left to the individual Christian.

It is clear that Luke in fact has poor non-Christians in mind as the recipients of alms. He looks upon the poor as "objects," so to speak, of the help given. This rather "objectivizing" attitude toward the poor recipients of alms suggests that in Luke's community there were no destitute (*ptōchoi*) individuals. For if the destitute are members of the community, it makes no sense for Luke to threaten the rich by saying that this group will be eschatological "substitutes" for those originally invited to the banquet in the heavenly *basileia* (Lk. 14:21-24). Luke is a theologian who is seriously concerned that Christians be merciful to these poor; if the latter are members of his community and are present before him, how can he treat them as a group not originally invited, who will replace respected folk at the heavenly banquet?

Also relevant here is the fact that while Luke takes over the Marcan story of the anointing of Jesus, he recasts it as the story of the woman who is a great sinner (Mk. 14:2-11//Lk. 7:36-50). In Mark's story the objection is raised that the woman has wasted a costly ointment, which might have been sold for about 300 denarii and the proceeds distributed to the poor. To this Jesus answers, "Let her alone; why do you trouble her? She has done a good deed to me. For you always have the poor with you, and whenever you will, you can do good to them; but you will not always have me" (Mk. 14:6f, RSV modified). Luke does not repeat this verse. The fact that it militates against his focus on mercy to the poor is surely not the only reason. Another and more important reason is probably the statement, "You always have the poor with you." He must omit this observation precisely because there are no poor in his community. In his community there are very likely ordinary folk, but none who are destitute (*ptōchoi*). The key word *ptōchos* ("poor") does not occur in Acts; it is replaced by *endeēs* ("needy," 4:34).

Finally, Luke's use of *diakonia* ("support, assistance") is a further argument for our thesis that when he uses the term "almsgiving" he has poor non-Christians in mind. For when he speaks of supplying the primitive Jerusalem community with daily food and of assisting the Christians of Judea who are threatened by famine (Acts 6:1ff.; 11:29), he uses the term "support" or "assistance," and not "alms." On the other hand, the assistance that Paul wishes to bring to his *nation* is called "alms" (Acts 24:17).

Eleēmosynē ("alms") thus has for its recipients the poor who are not members of the Christian community: for example, beggars, the blind, the lame, the crippled. One form of almsgiving is for Christians to invite these people to their tables. Those who do so will be rewarded at the resurrection of the just (Lk. 14:7-14).

Looking back over the material supplied by Luke's exhortations we find, on the one hand, the demand for a renunciation of half of a person's possessions and, on the other, the demand for charity toward the poor who do not belong to the community. The texts to be reviewed in the next section will show that Luke also has strong ideas about caritative activity within the community.

3. Caritative Activity within the Community

Whenever Luke turns to caritative activity within the community, the controlling idea seems to be the one expressed by Paul in his farewell address to the elders of Ephesus: "I coveted no one's silver or gold or apparel. You yourselves know that these hands ministered to my necessities, and to those who were with me. In all things I have shown you that by so toiling one must help the weak, remembering the words of the Lord Jesus, how he said, 'It is more blessed to give than to receive' " (Acts 20:33-35). Paul's formulation—to help the economically weak (*asthenountes*) in obedience to the Lord's words: to give is more blessed than to receive—can be taken as programmatic for Luke's conception of caritative activity within the community.

The context of Paul's exhortation makes it clear that the reference is to behavior within the community. He is delivering a farewell address to a chosen group of Christians (the elders), in which he also urges them to watchfulness in regard to external attacks on the community and to erroneous teaching within the community (vv. 28–31). He presents himself as a model. He has not coveted money or clothing, but on the contrary has worked both for himself and for his fellow workers.

The most important description of this caritative activity within the community is given in the part of Jesus' Sermon on the Plain that begins with the command of love of enemies. We turn now to a detailed examination of this passage.

LUKE'S INTERPRETATION OF LOVE OF ENEMIES

The section of the Sermon on the Plain that begins with the command to love our enemies is addressed, as we showed earlier, to a crowd that includes both Jews and pagans and is probably intended to represent the later church (Lk. 6:17). This section is clearly set apart as a unit by the verses that frame it (6:27a; 7:1); it includes verses 27b–49 of chapter 6. The passage as it stands in Luke is not to be understood in terms of the historical situation either of Jesus himself or of the Sayings-source, although important elements in the discourse come from this complex of traditions. On the contrary, the passage, like the other texts we have analyzed, must be interpreted in light of their context in Luke or, as required, of the social situation of the community for which Luke is writing.

Luke explains the command of love of enemies as an exhortation to prosperous and respected Christians. They are to do good to their fellow Christians, even if the latter hate them. They are to exercise charity without expecting a return: to lend, for example, without demanding a return of what was loaned, or to lend without expecting a full repayment, or to cancel debts. This thesis may at first sight seem puzzling, since we usually think of love of enemies as a specific kind of social intercourse and not behavior that has to do with problems of debts and loans. Our interpretation is based on the following observations.

In verse 35 Luke sums up his interpretation of the command of love of enemies: "But love your enemies, and do good, and lend, expecting nothing in return; and your reward will be great, and you will be sons of the Most High; for he is kind to the ungrateful and selfish." He is here setting disparate notions side by side: love of enemies and doing good or lending money (*dameizein*). Matthew, on the other hand, retains the original meaning of love of enemies when he accompanies the command with an exhortation: "and pray for those who persecute you" (Mt. 5:44). Luke introduces his interpretation of the command as relating to caritative behavior at the very start of the passage: "Love your enemies, do good to those who hate you" (6:27b).

These alterations in the context as found in the Sayings-source, where the problem of love of enemies was alone originally thematized, make clear the thrust of Luke's interpretation. His main interest is in the challenge to do good. This is also clear from the way in which corresponding concepts from Hellenistic ethics are piled up in this section of the sermon: *kalōs poiein* or *agathopoiein* ("do good"); *agathos* or *agathos anthropos* ("good" or "good person"); and *thēsauros agathos* ("good treasure"). Then again, the concluding verses repeat the exhortation to activity. Finally, Luke distinguishes the rules of behavior that he has formulated from the kind of ethical practice found among "sinners" (6:32–36). There can thus be no doubt but that Luke interprets Jesus' command of love of enemies as referring to the problem of doing good.

The programmatic statement—in Luke's version, "Do good to those who hate you"—at the beginning of Jesus' discourse on love of enemies is formulated in such a way that it gives rise to two questions: What concrete good deeds does Luke expect? Who are to practice this behavior, and who are the recipients of the good deeds?

To begin with, it is clear that Luke is in principle speaking to Christians. The confession of Jesus as *Kyrios* ("Lord") is presupposed (6:46); so too is the idea of God as Father (6:36), which, when taken in conjunction with the confession of Jesus as Lord, is an idea Christians alone can have. It is also immediately evident that the addressees of these ethical admonitions are "superior" Christians, that is, those in a position to do the kind of thing being asked; for example, to lend without expecting full repayment (6:34). Moreover, the Christians being addressed are not only economically superior; they also feel themselves to be morally superior. This is shown by verses 39–42, in which all three images (the blind leader of the blind; the teacher; the man who wants to remove the speck from his brother's eye) are meant for Christians who regard themselves as better than others. Their claim to superiority is ironically accepted. That they feel superior to other Christians is clear in particular from the image of the speck in a brother's eye.

Luke is therefore telling prosperous and respectable Christians that they are to do good to the economically weaker members of the community. But it is not enough to say that the recipients of the good deeds are economically weaker. The people in question are socially as well as economically on a lower level than the respectable Christians being addressed. In other words, Luke is not asking prosperous Christians of the respectable type to do good to other respectable Christians who have suffered economic losses. Such an interpretation is already excluded by the three comparisons just mentioned. The brothers to whom good is to be done are economically needy but also less esteemed by those being addressed.

Confirmation of the interpretation thus far given is provided by the reason that Luke offers for his demands. This reason is given with special vividness in 6:32–34: "If you love those who love you, what credit is that to you? For even sinners love those who love them. And if you do good to those who do good to you, what credit is that to you? For even sinners do the same. And if you lend to those from whom you hope to receive, what credit is that to you? Even sinners lend to sinners, to receive as much again."

The ethic here described, from which Luke distinguishes the kind of behavior he is calling for, typifies the social intercourse that is usual among equals at this period. Luke presupposes that precisely this outlook controls the invitations people give to dinners in their homes (see 14:12-14), and he is critical of it. Instead of inviting relatives, friends, and rich neighbors, hosts should invite the destitute to their tables. Such peoples are unable to repay (*antapodounai*) them, and therefore they will be rewarded at the resurrection of the just. As in the context of "love of enemies," so here Luke expects that the usual practice based on return of favors will be abandoned. Instead of acting according to that kind of ethical code, respected and prosperous Christians are to "do good" and "lend" without expecting a return (6:35). In the context of "love of enemies" a heavenly reward again awaits those who abandon the usual practice (v. 35). The usual practice among equals is reflected in, for example, Jesus son of Sirach: "He that shows mercy will lend to his neighbor, and he that strengthens him with his hand keeps the commandments. Lend to your neighbor in time of his need; and in turn, repay your neighbor promptly. Confirm your word and keep faith with him, and on every occasion you will find what you need" (Sir. 29:1ff.).

Luke describes the usual practice of exchanging favors among equals as the practice of *hamartōloi* ("sinners"). But he is not interested in describing the ethical behavior he is calling for as peculiarly Christian and contrasting it with that of "pagans." That is, he is not interested in an abstract ethical claim that Christians might make as opposed to non-Christians. The concept *hamartōlos* never conveys such a meaning in Luke. Sinners are here described in terms of their social behavior: "sinner" refers to the condition of human life prior to *metanoia* ("conversion") and implies no specific difference between Christian and pagan.

Luke is thus calling for the abandonment of an ethical practice customary at that time, according to which people do good to their equals in the expectation of receiving something in return.[42] He expects respected and prosperous Christians to do good even to those in social classes inferior to their own. Otherwise they will be blind leaders of the blind: people who feel superior to those they despise but who in fact have themselves not understood the demand made of them by Jesus, namely, to be merciful. In Lk. 14:12-14 it is destitute non-Christians who profit by the behavior called for; in the context of Luke's interpretation of love of enemies, those who profit are Christians looked down upon by his addressees.

The demands made by Luke show that the recipients in question are needy but not poor. Prosperous and respected Christians are to lend money (*dameizein*), even when they cannot expect to receive "an equal amount" (*ta isa*) in return (6:34). The reference here is not to professional money-lending, with which Luke is also familiar (see 19:23), since there is no question of interest or profit. The reference is, rather, to a nonprofessional loan made with the risk or danger that the lender will not receive an equal amount in return.

In the passage cited above from Jesus son of Sirach, the author urges solidarity among equals, who are to lend to one another in time of need. He expects the giver to receive a similar loan if the need should arise. In this context, the lender is also to make loans at risk and be patient if the borrower cannot repay within the appointed time (see Sir. 29:1ff.). Luke, on the other hand, supposes that the borrower may not be able to pay back (fully) and is thinking not of the exceptional situation in which a person suffers economic distress but of the situation in which by reason of one's customary economic situation the person needs loans and cannot repay them (fully). The creditor then cannot expect an earthly return in times of need, but will be rewarded by God.

Luke 6:30 argues along the same lines: "Give [*repeatedly*] to *every one* who begs from you; *and of him who takes away your goods do not ask them again.*" The words in italics are Luke's additions to Mt. 5:42. Luke supposes a situation in which the giver is not repaid the loan, so that according to legal stipulations then in force the borrower commits theft. Therefore, even though the giver has the right to demand back what was loaned and, if need be, can even use coercion, the giver is to renounce such action. In addition, Luke calls for a repeated giving (*didou*), and this to everyone (*panti*). A little further on, he repeats the exhortation to give: "give, and it will be given to you; good measure, pressed down, shaken together, running over, will be put into your lap. For the measure you give will be the measure you get back" (v. 38). Here it is clear once again that Luke expects the reward of giving to come from God.

We may therefore also expect—especially in light of the foregoing interpretation—that in Lk. 6:30 the principle of an exchange of favors among equals is once again being set aside. On the one hand, Luke asks for renunciation of any recourse to law in order to recover what was loaned. On the other hand, the addressees are to give not only within their own social class but to everyone who asks, and therefore also to brethren of whom the giver may have a low opinion. Finally, the one who loans is to cancel debts; our previous observations impose this interpretation of verse 37c with its verb *apolyein* ("release, pardon").

Luke thus refers the demand for love of enemies to the caritative activity of Christians among themselves. In this commandment he asks respected and prosperous Christians to do good to the needy brethren they look down upon, even if the latter hate them. The rich are to be *oiktirmōn* ("merciful"), as the heavenly Father is merciful (Lk. 6: 36). The kind of ethical behavior Luke looks for is a departure from the usual practice of good deeds among equals. The process reflected in this interpretation is not an exception in Luke. He approaches the command of love of neighbor in a similar manner. That is, here as in the commandment of love of enemies his concern is with the doing or practice of the commandment (see Lk. 10:28).

The question of who is to be understood by "neighbor" (*plesion*) was a debated one. Luke's point of departure in defining this concept is the person who is in need. The Samaritan was a neighbor to the man who had fallen among thieves (see Lk. 10:36f.); he showed mercy to the victim. In the commandment of love of enemies, Luke again takes as his point of departure the person who is in difficulty; here again he calls for mercy. In this context Luke is in a sense once again dealing with the problem of the "neighbor," as raised by the current practice of limiting the exchange of good deeds to one's equals. If mercy plays a determining role in observing the commandment of love of neighbor, then even more does it determine the behavior of which Luke speaks in connection with the commandment of love of enemies.

VI. LUKE'S CONCRETE SOCIAL UTOPIA

Luke has in mind a group that lives as an independent community in a city of the Roman empire (though not in Palestine). It evidently does not have members who belong to the upper class, but neither does it have members among the destitute (beggars, etc.). There are nonetheless serious tensions within the community. These are caused, on the one hand, by economic differences: in addition to rich people there are others who are in need, ordinary folk such as tax collectors, manual workers, and the like. On the other hand, there are also social tensions. Respected and respectable Christians look down on the ordinary people, especially when the latter have a reputation for engaging in illegal dealings (tax collectors, soldiers). As is generally the case in the Roman empire, social distinctions are not necessarily identical with economic distinctions. A rich man like Zacchaeus, a chief tax collector, can easily be one of those upon whom the respectable look down.

Luke formulates his Christian social ethics to meet the social situation of his community. The call for compassion to the wretched and needy is fundamental. Especially under the rubric of *eleēmosynē* ("alms"), it is inculcated upon all Christians and refers specifically to help given to the poorest of the poor—who probably do not belong to the community itself. These people are the "objects" of charity, but no longer, as they had been in the earliest tradition, the active agents of the Christian message. We today are accustomed to drawing a contrast between caritative aid, thought of as a drop in the ocean, and demands for radical alteration of the social situation. Such a contrast may be appropriate in our present historical context, but it does not do justice to the situation of Luke. In his world, unlike the world of Palestine and the Diaspora communities, compassion shown in caritative works was something exceptional. The first need, therefore, was to create an awareness of the need for such compassion.

This general call for compassion toward those in distress is probably directed even to the ordinary folk of the Christian community; to the extent possible, they too are to give this kind of help. But the primary thing Luke expects from them is that they should abandon any illegal behavior. Their conversion is to manifest itself especially in a turning away from activities that are against the law.

At the center of the social message of Jesus in Luke are the instructions given to the rich and respectable. The case of Zacchaeus, the despised chief tax collector, gives them an example to be followed: renunciation of half of their possessions. The duty of the prosperous is not to gather treasure for themselves, but to become rich in God's sight, that is, to be charitable and take the side of the weak. The reference is especially to the needy within the community. There the renunciation of half of one's possessions becomes a standard that gives guidance to the rich. Detailed requirements are then provided in Luke's interpretation of the commandment of love of enemies. The prosperous should give to everyone who asks and make no demand for a return; they should make risky loans and cancel debts when dealing with the Christian brethren on whom they look down and who hate them in return. Only in this way can prosperous and respectable Christians live up to their claim of being leaders of the blind. For this claim requires that they be merciful, as the heavenly Father is merciful.

We mentioned earlier that Luke has been classified as a writer who is "very much a socialist thinker."[43] It is always risky, of course, to transfer modern social utopias and political programs to an ancient setting. Nonetheless, if we are to think in categories at all, that description of Luke's concern seems more adequate than the description of him as "evangelist of the poor." This he is not. The poor (in the sense of the destitute) are not the focus of his attention, nor is his social program identical with an ethic of undifferentiated almsgiving. He can more correctly be called the "evangelist of the rich." This does not mean that he is their pastor who makes the message "Jesus, hope of the poor" attractive to them. It means, rather, that he is an exceptionally keen critic of the rich and wants their conversion, which is possible only by way of radical renunciation (renunciation of half of their possessions) and unpleasant specific actions (risky loans, cancellation of debts, gifts).

Over and above this, Luke has a concrete social goal in view: an equal distribution of property within the community. He is far from offering a political program for a comprehensive redistribution of property throughout society. He does, however, have a program, but it is for the Christian community. In his picture of the first Christian community in Jerusalem, he formulates his own utopian vision of a Christian community that is characterized by material and social equality.

The textual basis for this assertion is the disputed passages in Acts (2:41–47; 4:32–37), which describe what has been called a "communism inspired by love." The two passages do not give a historically faithful account of the primitive Jerusalem community, but neither are they simply idealizations of it on Luke's part. Rather, on the basis of information about the primitive community that we can no longer reconstruct, Luke here paints a picture of a Christian community as he thinks it should be. In other words, the circumstances described here reflect the situation in the Lucan community and turn this into a picture of what Luke thinks this community should be. The picture of the primitive community thus takes what actually was (as Luke sees it) and uses it to show how things should be. But it also shows that what should be does not exist at present. The picture of the original community does not simply describe a theoretically possible ideal state (one chosen at random, as it were);

rather, the ideal has its concrete background in the deficiencies of Luke's present community—at least as Luke sees it.

Scholars have often pointed out that in his accounts of the primitive community Luke is conflating Old Testament and Greek communal ideals. The key word *koinōnia* ("communion, fellowship"), the remarks on the communal use of property (e.g., "all . . . had all things in common" [*panta koina*]), and the description of the ideal community (e.g., "one heart and soul" [*kardia kai psychē mia*]) are found, even if not always together, in some of the Greek philosophers (we need think only of Plato and Aristotle).[44] All three key ideas occur in Iamblichus' biography of Pythagoras.[45] The idea that "there was not a needy person among them" (Acts 4:34) may very well be based on Deut. 15:4.[46]

As a matter of fact, Luke describes the ideal circumstances of the primitive community in such a way that a Hellenistic reader is likely to recall the Greek ideal of friendship. But the interpretation of the passages in Acts is not advanced by drawing analogies between Luke's descriptions and comparable ideas. The reason is that Luke is not describing an unattainable ideal. His intention is to describe what has actually taken place in the past, but he draws the elements of the picture from Greek utopian visions of society. He holds up this past as a mirror for his own community and hopes the latter will be guided by it.

This interpretation is confirmed by the fact that the dissolution (not explicitly mentioned) of that communion of friendship did not have solely external causes. Rather, external forces (see Acts 8:1, the dispersal of the community's members) combined with erosions within the community. The latter, moreover, are typical of what is attacked in the social gospel of Luke. Thus immediately after the second account of the ideal situation in the primitive community, and in clear contrast to Barnabas' exemplary behavior, Luke describes the negative example given by Ananias and Sapphira (Acts 5:1-11). The love of money shown by this couple undermines the communion based on love.

The "murmuring" of the "Hellenists" against the "Hebrews," because the widows of the former were neglected in the daily distribution, is probably to be explained along the same lines (Acts 6:1ff.). It seems that the widows of the "Hellenists" were neglected, that is, not taken into account, in the distribution of food to the needy of the community. And there was probably no ill will at work in this. The fact that these widows belonged to the "Hellenists" indicates, rather, that they were part of a group of people in Jerusalem who were not, in principle, to be reckoned among the needy. It is true, of course, that the distinction between "Hellenists" and "Hebrews" was based on a difference in language spoken: the one group spoke Greek, the other Aramaic.[47] But a social distinction, at least in principle, seems also to be latent. For in the Roman province the Greek-speaking neighborhoods were made up mostly of prosperous and respectable people. Evidence of this is the fact that they were usually the first to receive Roman citizenship.[48] If we suppose this situation to be also in the background of Luke's account of the opposition between Greek-speaking and Aramaic-speaking Christians, then here again it would be the respectable and prosperous who were undermining the ideal community, as those other prosperous Christians, Ananias and Sapphira, had done.

These two negative examples help to illumine the positive ideal at work in the primitive community: common, not private use of property; spiritual communion (unanimity).

The description "communism based on love" is misleading. For while Luke gives ambiguous descriptions of communal ownership (e.g., *panta koina* ["everything in common"]), his meaning is clear: private property benefited the entire community. Possessors of property (lands and houses) sold it and gave the proceeds to the apostles. The money was then given to those who needed it, so that there was now no one in need in the community (Acts 4:34f.). The selling and the distribution of proceeds are described as actions done once and for all. There is thus no reason for assuming that they were done in case after case, whenever someone was in need. In any event, the selling and distribution were in the interests of an equalization of ownership among Christians. Moreover, as the story of Ananias and Sapphira makes clear, it was all voluntary. We cannot and should not try to imagine in detail how this equalization took place. Luke's interest is in the fact that it did occur. He evidently thinks of the equalization in simple arithmetical terms: possessors renounced enough to ensure that there were no longer either rich or needy people in the community.

The second important element in the positive ideal is the unanimity of the primitive community. It is a community in which, at the beginning, there are no longer any social tensions but, rather, one heart and one soul. The members are always together; they join in prayer in the temple, and they go from house to house celebrating the Eucharist (Acts 2:46). *Kata'oikon* ("from house to house; in their various private homes") probably means that Christians who were neighbors took turns opening their homes (since 3,000 or possibly 5,000 Christians could hardly fit into a single home) (Acts 2:41; 4:4).

Here again Luke probably has in mind some abuse in his own community, behind which lurks the same problem as behind the positive depiction of unanimity: namely, social tensions between the respectable and those on whom they look down. That is the situation in Luke's community; in the original community, on the contrary, there had been one heart and one soul. In Luke's community people meet in only a few houses of a Christian neighborhood (because the respectable will not enter the homes of those they looked down on?); in the primitive community they had simply gone from home to home in turn.

Luke has already made it clear in this Gospel how important he regards the Lord's Supper as a communal meal. There, on occasion of the "institution" of the Lord's Supper by Jesus, Luke says simply: "And he took a cup, and when he had given thanks he said, 'Take this, and divide it among yourselves' " (Lk. 22:17). In the primitive community, as Luke describes it, the Lord's Supper was accompanied by a regular meal. He calls attention to the fact that this regular meal was marked by "jubilation" and "purity of heart" (Acts 2:46). *Aphelotēs* ("purity") is to be understood here as "simplicity" and means that those present ate what they needed and there was no gluttony and no drinking sessions (cf. Lk. 21:34; 1 Cor. 11:20ff.). In the context of Luke's work, the "jubilation" of the community is meant to recall the joyous feast that was celebrated after the return of the lost son and in which the elder brother should have taken part (see Lk. 15:23, 32; see also Lk. 19:6). For Luke, joyous fellowship brings home in a vivid way the solidarity that should exist among Christians. "Murmuring" is what is actually to be found in his community (see Lk. 5:30; 15:1f.; 19:7). It is easy to see that the depiction of life in the primitive community is directly related to the concrete situation in Luke's own community.

Luke had to translate the message of hope for the poor, which the disciples of Jesus had preached once in Palestine, so that it would apply to the much changed social situation in his own community. In his view the following of Jesus takes concrete form in the solidarity of those whose divergent social and material circumstances would of themselves produce only hatred and destruction.

Notes

We decided that it was impossible to eliminate notes entirely. Their function is to show where our statements can be checked and to refer interested readers to sources where they can acquire further information on the questions raised. Only in exceptional cases will it be possible to offer an explicit discussion of other modern interpretations of the texts used. Readers who have in front of them divergent interpretations of the texts will generally find that we make clear the reasons for the interpretation we have chosen. This study is the result of joint work, and we accept joint responsibility for it. Chapters 1 and 2 were written by Luise Schottroff, and chapter 3 by Wolfgang Stegemann.—L.S. AND W.S.

CHAPTER 1

1. E.g., Josephus, *Jewish War* 5, 449–51: mass crucifixion of Jewish deserters by Titus before the walls of Jerusalem; ibid., 2, 75 (*Antiquities* 17, 293): mass crucifixion of 2,000 rebels by Varus; ibid., 2, 241 (*Antiquities* 20, 129): crucifixion of prisoners of war by Quadratus at Caesarea. For further details, see Martin Hengel, *Crucifixion in the Ancient World and the Folly of the Message of the Cross,* trans. John Bowden (Philadelphia, Pa.: 1976).

2. Rudolf Bultmann, "The Primitive Christian Kerygma and the Historical Jesus," in C. E. Braaten, ed., *The Historical Jesus and the Kerygmatic Christ: Essays on the New Question of the Historical Jesus* (Nashville, Tenn.: Abingdon, 1964), p. 24.

3. Martin Kähler, *The So-called Historical Jesus and the Historic, Biblical Christ,* trans. C. E. Braaten (Philadelphia, Pa.: Fortress Press, 1964).

4. Ernst Käsemann, "The Problem of the Historical Jesus," in his *Essays on New Testament Themes,* trans. W. J. Montague (Studies in Biblical Theology; London: SCM Press, 1954), pp. 15–47.

5. The method for getting at this will be described in sec. III.1 of this chapter.

6. L. Friedländer, *Darstellunger aus der Sittengeschichte Roms,* 4 vols. (Leipzig, 1922; reprinted, Aalen, 1964); Adolph von Harnack, *The Mission and Expansion of Christianity in the First Three Centuries,* trans. J. Moffatt, 2 vols. (New York: G. Putnam's Sons, 1908).

7. Especially Jeremias's *Jerusalem in the Time of Jesus: An Investigation into Economic and Social Conditions during the New Testament Period,* trans. F. H. and C. H. Cave (Philadelphia, Pa.: Fortress Press, 1969).

8. Fernando Belo, *A Materialist Reading of the Gospel of Mark,* trans. Matthew J. O'Connell (Maryknoll, N.Y.: Orbis Books, 1981), pp. 241ff.

9. It is also important, of course, to analyze Mark and Matthew in order to discover their special ways of following Jesus. But such a discussion would have made this book overly long.

10. This interpretation is generally accepted by biblical scholars today.

11. Gunther Bornkamm, *Jesus of Nazareth,* trans. I. and F. McLuskey, with James M. Robinson (New York: Harper & Row, 1960), p. 81.

12. H. Braun, "Gott, die Eröffnung des Lebens für die Nonkonformisten: Erwägungen zu Mk 2, 15–17," in *Festschrift für E. Fuchs* (Tübingen, 1973), pp. 97ff.

13. Bornkamm, *Jesus of Nazareth,* p. 74.

14. Braun, "Gott, die Eröffnung, " and Braun, *Jesus* (Stuttgart, 1969), especially p. 144.

15. Bornkamm, *Jesus of Nazareth,* p. 79.

16. On the *portatorium,* see below in the text. The concept of *telōnēs* ("tax collector") could also be used in a much broader sense of anyone who had a lease from the state. E.g., even a fisherman who leased fishing rights from the state and was bound to pay one twenty-fifth of his profits could be called a *telōnēs*; see R. Taubenschlag, *The Law of Greco-Roman Egypt in the Light of the Papyri* (Warsaw, 1955), pp. 664f. For further data on the situation of tax collectors, see especially O. Michel, *"telōnēs," TDNT* 8:88ff., and F. Vettinghoff, in A. F. Pauly and G. Wissowa, *Realencyclopaedie der Classischen Altertuswissenschaft,* 68 vols. (1953), 43:346ff.

17. On the misconduct of tax collectors, see below, in text.

18. *Corpus iuris civilis,* Dig. 39, 4, 9.

19. Josephus, *Jewish War* 2, 287 and 292.

20. See the edition of the various versions in H. Gressmann, *Vom reichen Mann und armen Lazarus* (Berlin, 1918), pp. 70ff.

21. The terminology *telōnēs/architelōnēs* in the sense indicated is not attested elsewhere, but the situation that required the distinction between principal and subordinate tax collectors was widespread; see, e.g., B. bSab 78b.

22. F. Vettinghoff, in Pauly-Wissowa, *Realencyclopaedie,* 43: 348.

23. This is a secular analogy for the tithe on herbs in Mt. 23:23 par.

24. Aramaic and Greek texts of the Tariff in CIS II, 3 (1926), no. 3913. There is an old English translation of the Tariff in G. A. Cooke, ed., *A Text-Book of North-Semitic Inscriptions* (Oxford: Clarendon Press, 1903), pp. 313ff. It is clear from these texts that our concept of "tax" is far from covering what was understood in the contexts with which we are dealing.

25. Tacitus, *Annals* XIII, 51.

26. This is assumed by M. Rostovtsev, *Geschichte der Staatspacht* (1902; Rome, 1971), pp. 343f., 480. See also Taubenschlag, *Law of Greco-Roman Egypt,* p. 553; D. Nörr, "Die Evangelien des Neuen Testaments und die sogenannte hellenistische Rechtskoine," *Zeitschrift der Savigny-Stiftung für Rechtsgeschichte,* Romanist. Abt. 78 (1961): 134.

27. So little do the legal cases and principles of reimbursement in Lev. 5:20ff.; Ex. 21:37ff.; 1 Sam. 12:6 apply to Lk. 19:8 that one should regard the last-named not as an instance of voluntary and supererogatory restitution according to Old Testament rules, but as a normal legal procedure according to Roman law.

28. bNed 28a; see bBK 113a; probably also bSanh 25b. For more on the subject, see below in text.

29. Julius Pollux, *Onomasticon* IX, 32.

30. Plutarch, *De curiositate* 7 (*Moralia* 518E).

31. Philostratus, *Vita Apollonius* I, 20.

32. Xenophon, *Oeconomicus* IV, 2f.; trans. C. Lord, in L. Strauss, *Xenophon's Socratic Discourse: An Interpretation of the* Oeconomicus (Ithaca, N.Y.: Cornell University Press, 1970), p. 17.

33. Julius Pollux, *Onomasticon* VI, 128.

34. bNed 28a; see bBK 113a; probably also bSanh 25b.

35. See the legend of Ma'jan the (son of the) Tax Collector, in Billerbeck, II, 231f., and see Josephus, *Jewish War* 2, 287 and 292.

36. See the legend mentioned in n. 35, above.

37. Joachim Jeremias, "Zöllner und Sünder," *ZNTW* 30 (1931):293-300, especially p. 300. See also Jeremias, *Jerusalem in the Time of Jesus*, pp. 303ff., especially pp. 311f.

38. R. Meyer, "Der 'Am hā 'Ares: Ein Beitrag zur Religionssoziologie im ersten und zweiten nachchristlichen Jahrhundert," *Judaica* 3 (1947): 169-99.

39. Jeremias, *ZNTW* 30 (1931): 294.

40. Ibid., pp. 295, 300.

41. H. Herter, "Die Soziologie der antiken Prostitution im Lichte des heidnischen und christlichen Schrifttums," *JAC* 3 (1960): 79.

42. For an edition of the Palmyra Tariff, see n. 24, above.

43. There is evidence of brothels in Caesarea and Sebaste: Josephus, *Antiquities* 19, 357.

44. Dig. 5, 3, 7, sec. 1.

45. This could also happen to sons: Quintilian, *Institutio* VII, 1, 55.

46. For additional and comprehensive information, see the essay of H. Herter (cited in n. 41, above).

47. See, e.g., Aristophanes, *Plutus* 511, 532ff., where Poverty (Penia) says: "I sit like a Mistress, by Poverty's lash constraining the needy mechanic; when I raise it, to earn his living he'll turn, and work in a terrible panic . . . . My *poor* man, it is true, has to scrape and to screw, and his work he must never be slack in" (trans. B. Rogers, in *Aeschylus, Sophocles, Euripides, Aristophanes* [Great Books of the Western World 5; Chicago: Encyclopedia Britannica, 1952], p. 635).

48. In Jewish care of the poor, the distinction between local and outside beggars played an essential role. Beggars from elsewhere were to receive only absolutely necessary food (Billerbeck II, 644; see especially Pea VIII, 7).

49. Friedländer, *Darstellungen aus der Sittengeschichte Roms,* I, 159f.

50. Josephus, *The Jewish War,* trans. G. A. Williamson (Baltimore, Md.: Penguin Books, 1959), p. 157.

51. Josephus, *Jewish War* 3, 532-42. Further material on the economic context of the rebellions: *Jewish War* 4, 241; 7, 438. On the economic situation in Palestine in the first century, see S. Applebaum, "Economic Life in Palestine," in S. Safrai et al., *The Jewish People in the First Century,* vol. 2 (Compendium Rerum Judaicarum ad Novum Testamentum, Sect. I; Assen-Amsterdam, 1976), pp. 631ff.

52. Josephus, *Jewish War* 5, 567ff.; see also 3, 179; 6, 195; 6, 204.

53. For the situation in Tiberias, see Josephus, *Antiquities* 18, 36ff. On the reign of Herod, see Josephus, *Jewish War* 2, 84ff. (Williamson trans., p. 121), and *Antiquities* 15, 267ff. On famines, see Josephus, *Antiquities* 15, 299ff.; 20, 52; 20, 101.

54. "Flight for social reasons" is discussed below, in chap. 2.I.3.

55. For the method used here in dealing with the earliest tradition about Jesus, see also Luise Schottroff, "Das Magnificat und die älteste Tradition über Jesus von Nazareth," *EvTh* 38 (1978): 298ff.

56. See below, chap. 2, for all the evidence regarding the stages of tradition that preceded Q.

57. The oldest textual *form* of individual texts usually need not be discussed in detail.

The arguments for the oldest form of a text are treated at great length in the study of the form criticism and would be repetitious here. The commentary of H. Schürmann, *Das Lukasevangelium* (Freiburg, 1969), will provide the interested reader with a basic introduction to the arguments that play a part in the reconstruction of texts.

58. In the Beatitudes, poverty is to be understood as an economic and social condition, not as an ethical or religious outlook. Luke 6:20f. is not an exhortation, not even an implicit one. Fundamental studies of this question include E. Percy, *Die Botschaft Jesu* (Lund, 1953); L. E. Keck, "The Poor among the Saints in the New Testament," *ZNTW* 56 (1965): 100ff.; 57 (1966): 54ff.; E. Bammel, "Ptōchos," *TDNT* 6:885ff. The decisive argument for the meaning of the word "poor" in Lk. 6:20f. is provided by the immediate context, namely, the second and third Beatitudes. The tradition of interpretation of the concept outside the New Testament is so diversified that it allows no compelling conclusion about the meaning of the word. On the other hand, given this broad and diversified conceptual tradition, we must say in general that even in texts in which "poverty" = "humility" or "poverty" = "piety," the devout or the humble are also poor (in the economic sense).

59. See the material in Rudolf Bultmann, *The Gospel of John: A Commentary*, trans. G. R. Beasley-Murray, R. W. N. Hoare, and J. K. Riches (Philadelphia: Westminster Press, 1971), pp. 505-7.

60. See especially K. Reploh, *Markus-Lehrer der Gemeinde* (Stuttgart, 1969), pp. 191-201.

61. J. Wellhausen, *Das Evangelium Marci* (Berlin, 1909), p. 81, considered v. 25b to be a secondary addition. Some exegetes regard the word *plousios* ("rich man") as a later substitute for an original *anthropos* ("man"); see, e.g., N. Walter, *ZNTW* 53 (1962): 210; similarly, E. Jüngel, *Paulus und Jesus* (Tübingen, 1967), p. 183; W. Harnisch, in *Festschrift E. Fuchs* (Tübingen, 1973), p. 167.

62. This and other passages of the Ethiopic Apocalypse of Enoch are from the translation by E. Isaac, in *The Old Testament Pseudepigrapha*, vol. 1: *Apocalyptic Literature and Testaments*, ed. by J. H. Charlesworth (Garden City, N.Y.: Doubleday, 1983), pp. 13-89.

63. On this text, see below, chap. 3.II.3, for further discussion.

64. Thus J. Schniewind, *Das Evangelium nach Markus* (Göttingen, 1949), p. 139; Joachim Jeremias, *The Parables of Jesus*, trans, S. H. Hooke (rev. ed.; New York: Scribner, 1963), p. 36 n. 47.

65. E.g., Hesiod, *Works and Days* V, 1ff.; Sir. 10:8ff.

66. This and other passages of the Syriac Apocalypse of Baruch are from the translation by A. F. J. Klijn in *The Old Testament Pseudepigrapha* I, 621-52. Collections of material on this theme are cited in, e.g., B. Gatz, *Weltalter, goldene Zeit und sinnverwandte Vorstellungen* (Hildesheim, 1967), pp. 48-51.

67. "First" as a description of rank (= "leading") in, e.g., Mk. 6:21; for further material, see W. Michaelis, "Prōtos," *TDNT* 6:868.

68. H. Gressmann, *Vom reichen Mann und armen Lazarus*, pp. 70ff.

69. German translation in E. Brunner-Traut, *Altägyptische Märchen* (1965), pp. 192ff.; see also the translation by G. Möller in the appendix, pp. 62ff., of Gressmann's book, *Vom reichen Mann*. The papyrus, in demotic script, is from the second half of the first century A.D.

70. The quotation opening the paragraph is a funerary inscription of the late Egyptian period, cited in H. Bonnet, *Reallexikon der ägyptischen Religionsgeschichte* (Berlin, 1952), p. 340. For Gressmann, see *Vom reichen Mann*, p. 55.

71. E. Percy, *Die Botschaft Jesu*, pp. 93ff.

72. H. Bolkestein, *Wohltätigkeit und Armenpflege im vorchristlichen Altertum* (Utrecht, 1939), p. 409.

73. Gressmann, *Vom reichen Mann*, p. 51.

74. E.g., A. Jülicher, *Die Gleichnisreden Jesu* (Tübingen, 1910), vol. 2, pp. 635ff.

75. For the arguments in detail, see Luise Schottroff, "Das Magnificat . . . ," cited in n. 55, above.

76. See, e.g., E. Bammel, "Ptōchos,"*TDNT* 6:906, on Lk. 16:19ff.; the story, says Bammel, is Pre-New Testamental. For other judgments of the same kind, see below, chap.1.III.9.

77. See, e.g., L. Goppelt, "Peinaō," *TDNT* 6:17 n. 35. J. Becker, *Untersuchungen zur Entstehungsgeschichte der Testamente der zwölf Patriarchen* (Leiden, 1970), p. 324 n. 3, doubts the Christian origin of the interpolations and refers to Ethiopic Enoch 92ff. But the latter passage provides only a parallel *motif*, since there is no question there of a reversal of *social* destinies; it contributes nothing therefore to an understanding of Judah 25, 4, in the *Testaments of the Twelve Patriarchs*.

78. German translation in A. Wünsche, *Aus Israels Lehrhallen*, vol. 4 (Leipzig, 1909), pp. 218f. (= Jellinek, *Bet ha Midrasch* III, 22, 34).

79. Wünsche, *Aus Israels Lehrhallen*, p. 219; see Billerbeck III, 656f. On this passage, see Percy, *Die Botschaft Jesu*, pp. 75f.

80. See E. Bammel, "Ptōchos," *TDNT* 6:899-902; Percy, *Die Botschaft Jesu*, pp. 74-77; Billerbeck I, 818ff.; and Martin Hengel, *Property and Riches in the Early Church: Aspects of a Social History of Christianity*, trans. John Bowden (Philadelphia: Fortress Press, 1974), pp. 19-22.

81. The reversal of *social* destinies is often assumed to be asserted in Ethiopic Enoch 94ff.; see, e.g., P. Volz, *Die Eschatologie der jüdischen Gemeinde* (Tübingen, 1934), pp. 136f.; Hengel, *Property and Riches,* p. 18. For a different view, see Percy, *Die Botschaft Jesu*, pp. 65-68. The citations from Ethiopic Enoch that follow in the text are from the translation by E. Isaac, cited in n. 62, above.

82. On this point, see the material in Klaus Koch, *The Growth of the Biblical Tradition: The Form-Critical Method,* trans. S. M. Cupitt (New York: Scribner, 1969), pp. 6-8.

83. See Ernst Käsemann, "Die Anfänge christlicher Theologie," in his *Exegetische Versuche und Besinnungen,* vol. 2 (Göttingen, 1970), p. 99.

84. Koch, *Growth of the Biblical Tradition*, pp. 39ff., 59ff.

85. Gressmann, *Vom reichen Mann*, p. 57. Rudolf Bultmann, *The History of the Synoptic Tradition*, trans. J. Marsh (Oxford: Blackwell, 1963), p. 126.

86. Lucian, *Dialogues of the Dead*, 1 (Diogenes and Pollux), no. 3, trans. M. D. Macleod, in *Lucian*, vol. 7 (Loeb Classics, Cambridge, Mass.: Harvard Univ. Press, 1961).

87. On love for sinners in Luke, see above, chap. 1.II.1, and below, chap. 3.IV.1.

88. On this, see what was said above in chap. 1.II.3.

89. We need not decide to what extent Luke is the author of the material peculiar to him that portrays the friendly attitude of Jesus to tax collectors and sinners. The special character of the Lucan interpretation is clear even to those who assume that he is using an older tradition. He gives the theme a special inflection that is found only in his Gospel.

90. See also below, chap. 2.III.2.

91. See Joachim Jeremias, *The Parables of Jesus*, p. 125 n. 48.

92. See above, chap. 1.II.1.

93. There is an especially vivid depiction in bSanh 111 a–b: "When Moses ascended the height, he found the Holy One—Blessed be he!—sitting there and writing 'Patience!' Then Moses spoke to him: 'Lord of the world, patient with the devout!' But the Lord answered him: 'With sinners too.' Moses responded: 'May sinners perish!' The Lord: 'You will shortly see what it is you have demanded.' When the Israelites sinned, the Lord said to Moses: 'Did you not say to me: Patient only with the devout?' But Moses replied: 'Lord of the world, did you not say to me: With sinners too?' It is to this that the Scripture verse refers: 'Show your power to be great, O Lord, as you promised.' " See also E. Sjöberg, *Gott und die Sünder im palästinischen Judentum* (Stuttgart, 1939), especially p. 113.

94. Mark 2:17 should not be misinterpreted to mean that the position of the adversaries is described in the negative half of the sentence (God is there for the just and therefore *not* for sinners). Mark 2:17 employs the same logic as Mk. 2:27: the Pharisees do *not* mean that the human being is made for the sabbath. Both statements simply endeavor to clarify the position being maintained by contrasting it with its opposite. They are not polemical statements.

95. See Luise Schottroff, "Die Erzählung vom Pharisäer und Zöllner," in *Neues Testament und christliches Existenz: Festschrift für H. Braun* (Tübingen, 1973), pp. 439ff.

96. See also above, chap.1.II.1.

97. On this point, see especially O. Michel, "Telōnes," *TDNT* 8:104; Joachim Jeremias, "Der Gedanke des 'Heiligen Restes' im Spätjudentum und in der Verkündigung Jesu," *ZNTW* 42 (1949): 184–94; H. Braun, *Spatjüdischhäretischer und früchristlicher Radikalismus*, vol. 2 (Tübingen, 1957), pp. 18ff.

CHAPTER 2

1. In what follows we shall cite only the passages in Matthew for texts from the Sayings-source (Q). A "Q" following the citation indicates a reconstruction of the text in the Sayings-source on the basis of the parallel traditions in Matthew and Luke.

2. On the situation of dependent rural workers and small farmers, see A. Ben-David, *Talmudische Ökonomie*, vol. 1 (Hildesheim, 1974), pp. 58–72; on the minimum needed for survival , pp. 291–320. See also H. Kreissig, "Die landwirtschaftliche Situation in Palästina vor dem judäischen Krieg," *Acta Antiqua* 17 (1969): 223ff., especially pp. 249f.

3. Lucian, *Gallus* 22; Sir. 34:1–2; Plutarch, *De cupiditate divitiarum* (Moralia 523Cff.), passim.

4. On the ideal of the simple life in antiquity, see especially H. Hommel, "Das hellenistische Ideal vom einfachen Leben," *Studium Generale* 11 (1958): 742–51; R. Vischer, *Das einfache Leben* (Göttingen, 1965).

5. Epictetus, *Discourses* III, 26, trans. P. E. Matheson, in W. J. Oates, ed., *The Stoic and Epicurean Philosophers* (New York: Random House, 1940), p. 403.

6. Lucian's dialogue *Fugitivi,* from which the information is taken, provides further important material on these questions.

7. Ben-David, *Talmudische Ökonomie*, vol. 1, pp. 300f.

8. bSota 48. German trans. in S. Krauss, "Die Instruktion Jesu an die Apostel," *Angelos* 1 (1925): 101; see also Billerbeck 1, 439.

9. From the German trans. of the Q text by Adolph von Harnack, *Beiträge zur Einleitung in das Neue Testament*, vol. II: *Sprüche und Reden Jesu* (Leipzig, 1907).

10. From the German trans. by Harnack. On imprisonment for debt, see D. Norr, "Die Evangelien des Neuen Testaments und die sogennante hellenistische Rechtskoine," *Zeitschrift der Savigny-Stiftung für Rechtsgeschichte,* Romanist. Abt. 78 (1961), especially pp. 136ff.

11. M. Rostovtzeff, *Gesellschaft und Wirtschaft im römischen Kaiserreich,* vol. II (Leipzig, 1929), p. 65: "As a rule the villages remained silent in the first and second centuries."

12. Rudolf Bultmann, "Merimnaō," *TDNT* 4:591.

13. The justification of this reconstruction has often been repeated since Harnack made it, and need not be reproduced here. A collection of arguments is given in, e.g., S. Schulz, *Q: Die Spruchquelle der Evangelisten* (Zurich, 1972); on Lk. 12:4f., see E. Schweizer, "Psychē," *TDNT* 9:646–47.

14. Adolf von Deissmann, *Light from the Ancient East,* trans. L. M. R. Strachan (New York: George H. Doran, 1927), pp. 272ff.

15. Diogenes Laertius, *Lives of Eminent Philosophers* I, 51; trans. R. D. Hicks (Loeb Classics, Cambridge, Mass.: Harvard Univ. Press, 1959) vol. 1, p. 53.

16. On these anthropological problems, see especially G. Dautzenberg, *Sein Leben bewahren* (Munich, 1966), p. 94.

17. The reconstruction is based essentially on the convincing arguments of P. Hoffman, *Studien zur Theologie der Logienquelle* (Münster, 1972), pp. 236–311. For the Q version of the missionary discourse, the references to the parallel traditions will also be given (following an arrow) in the following discussion.

18. Billerbeck 1,574.

19. Ben-David, *Talmudische Ökonomie,* vol. 1, pp. 310–12; S. Krauss, *Talmudische Archäologie* (Leipzig, 1910), vol. I, pp. 134–36, 161, 167f., 604.

20. Examples of this interpretative approach in the history of scholarship are given in Hoffmann, *Studien,* pp. 320ff. From the methodological standpoint we agree fully with Hoffmann's own approach.

21. See especially J. Renger, "Flucht als soziales Problem in der altbabylonischen Gesellschaft," in *Gesellschaftsklassen im Alten Zweistromland und in den angrenzenden Gebieten* (18th Rencontre assyrologique internationale, Munich, June 29–July 3, 1972; Abhandlungen der Bayr. Akad. der Wiss., phil.-hist. Kl., N.F., H. 75; Munich, 1972), pp. 167–82. Under the rubric of "social uprooting," Gerd Theissen, " 'Wir haben alles verlassen' (Mc. X 28): Nachfolge und soziale Entwurzelung in der jüdisch-palästinischen Gesellschaft des. 1. Jahrhunderts n. Ch.," *NovTest* 19 (1977): 161–96, provides some material on flight for economic reasons in Palestine. Important evidence of itinerancy or vagabondage for social reasons in first-century Palestine is to be found in Josephus, *Antiquities* 18, 36ff., and *Jewish War* 3, 532ff. Luke 15:14 incidentally provides an exact description of the process of impoverishment: a man engages in day labor that no longer earns him enough to feed himself; he leaves the job and looks elsewhere for food.

22. Alongside Cynics who tried to live their ideals there were "Cynics" who were simply enthusiastic about these ideals and others who posed as wandering Cynic philosophers in order to exploit the prestige the latter enjoyed in society.

23. Lucian, *Cynicus* 6–8, trans. M. D. Macleod, in *Lucian,* vol. 8 (Loeb Classics, Cambridge, Mass.: Harvard Univ. Press, 1967), pp. 393–97.

24. Hoffman, *Studien,* pp. 326ff.

25. For discussion of the political interpretation Hoffmann puts on love of enemies in Q, see also chap. 2. I II.3, below.

26. Gerd Theissen, " 'Wir haben alles verlassen' " (n. 21, above), and "Wanderradi-

kalismus: Literatursoziologische Aspekte der Überlieferung von Worten Jesu im Urchristentum," *ZTK* 70 (1973): 245-71; see also his *Sociology of Early Palestinian Christianity,* trans. John Bowden (Philadelphia: Fortress Press, 1978).

27. Theissen, in *ZTK* (1973), p. 251; see also Theissen, *Sociology,* pp. 8ff.

28. Ibid., p. 259.

29. Theissen, in *NovTest* 19 (1977), p. 186.

30. Ibid., pp. 189-95.

31. See Theissen, *NovTest* 19 (1977), p. 185, and what is said about their afamilial ethos in *ZTK* (1973), p. 249, and the poverty ethos in *NovTest* (1977), pp. 177f.

32. On this point, see below, chap. 3.III.2.

33. For another view, see Hoffman, *Studien,* p. 223 n. 146, p. 302 n. 50.

34. From the German translation by P. Hoffmann, "Die Versuchungsgeschichte in der Logienquelle," *BZ* 13 (1969): 209.

35. Thus Billerbeck I, 87.

36. The argument that the temptation story represents a later Hellenistic stage of the Sayings-source because the Septuagint is used in it is not convincing. Traces of the Septuagint could have entered in the literary posthistory, that is, in the transmission of the text. Furthermore, the continuity of content between the other Q texts and this passage is too evident. Independently of the question of the use of the Septuagint, the *monō* in Mt. 4:10, Q has a substantive basis in the idea of God in Q, as has been shown. There is a good presentation of the question in P. Hoffmann's review of S. Schulz, *Q: Die Spruchquelle der Evangelisten,* in *BZ* 19 (1975): 104-15. On the not necessarily Hellenistic character of the title "Son of God," see Hoffmann, "Die Versuchungsgeschichte," p. 212.

37. Josephus, *Jewish War* 6, 311-13 (Williamson trans. [Baltimore, Md.: Penguin Books, 1959], p.350).

38. The arguments for the reconstruction are given in Schulz, *Q: Die Spruchquelle der Evangelisten,* pp. 442f.

39. As often in the parables, not too much can be based on the introductory sentence. In the context of the Sayings-source it is clear from what is said that this generation is being compared to children who do not respond to the shouts of the other children. For this interpretation, see, e.g., D. Zeller, "Die Bildlogik des Gleichnisses Mt. 11: 16 f./Lk. 7: 31f.," *ZNTW* 68 (1977): 252-57.

40. Hoffmann, *Studien,* p. 188.

41. The Sayings-source has no positive interest in the tradition of Jesus' love for tax collectors and sinners; see also below, n. 51 of this chapter.

42. For an example of a metaphorical interpretation of Mt. 10:38, Q, see Schulz' *Q: Die Spruchquelle der Evangelisten,* pp. 432f. The nonmetaphorical interpretation given here is based on the real historical context to which the Sayings-source belongs and which we know primarily from Josephus.

43. Josephus, *Jewish War* 6, 300ff., shows the Jewish leaders and the Romans collaborating in the torture of an embarrassing prophet. Crucifixions by the Romans at the instigation of Jewish collaborators are thus quite plausible.

44. Josephus, *Jewish War* 2, 338 and 417ff. The political location of the Sayings-source that is mentioned here is in Hoffmann, *Studien,* pp. 74ff., 332; Martin Hengel, *War Jesus revolutionär?* (Stuttgart, 1970), p. 22; O. H. Steck, *Israel und das gewaltsame Geschick der Propheten* (Neukirchen, 1967), p. 239.

45. *Ponēroi* was already used here in Q; see Lk. 6:35.

46. Moreover, Mt. 7:7-11, Q is certainly not an expression of "beggar's wisdom."

Theissen has too hastily isolated the first sentence from its immediate context here and its broader context in Q, and has related it to the situation of the wandering prophets (see his "Wanderradikalismus," p. 260).

47. For the reconstruction of the commandment of love of enemies in Q, see Luise Schottroff, "Gewaltverzicht und Feindesliebe," in *Festschrift für H. Conzelmann* (Tübingen, 1975), pp. 213f.

48. See W. Schottroff, *Der altisraelitische Fluchspruch* (Neukirchen, 1969), especially pp. 206-10.

49. Cf. Mt. 3:9, Q; 22:1-14, Q. For discussion of the significance of the mission to the pagans in Q, see the debate between D. Lührmann, *Die Redaktion der Logienquelle* (Neukirchen, 1969), and Schulz, Q: *Die Spruchquelle des Evangelisten,* in regard to the texts mentioned here.

50. Martin Luther King, Jr., "Loving Your Enemies," in his *Strength to Love* (New York: Pocket Books, 1964), pp. 48-49.

51. In the Sayings-source the straying sheep must be regarded as a metaphor for the Jews who reject the message of Jesus. In our opinion the Sayings-source does not have any further positive interest in tax collectors and sinners in Israel. The Q prophets have heard of Jesus' love for sinners (and therefore of the earliest Jesus tradition) primarily in the form of reproaches uttered by Jesus himself (see above, on Mt. 11:19f., Q). In Q the parable of the great banquet is likewise not related to the saving of the tax collectors and sinners but to the invitation given to the pagans once those originally invited (Israel) have failed to come. In opposition to the interpretation given here, Schultz Q: *Die Spruchquelle des Evangelisten,* regards the lost sheep as a metaphor for tax collectors and sinners (see especially p. 379).

52. Josephus, *Jewish War* 6, 300-309 (Williamson trans., pp. 349-50). On Jeshua, son of Ananias, see especially R. Meyer, *Der Prophet aus Galiläa* (Leipzig, 1940), pp. 46-48, and the notes in Josephus, *De bello judaico* II, 2, trans. into German by O. Michel and O. Bauernfeind (Darmstadt, 1969).

CHAPTER 3

1. R. W. Pohlmann, *Geschichte der sozialen Frage und des Sozialismus in der antiken Welt* (Munich, 1925), vol. 2, p. 470.

2. H.-J. Degenhardt, *Lukas, Evangelist der Armen* (Stuttgart, 1865).

3. C. Rogge, *Der irdische Besitz im Neuen Testament* (Göttingen, 1897).

4. E.g., by connecting the Beatitude of the poor with the disciples; on this, see below, chap. 3.II.

5. We are repeatedly struck by the way in which various kinds of demands—e.g., complete renunciation of possessions, partial renunciation of possessions, and even almsgiving—are juxtaposed.

6. On this, see above, chap. 2, introductory material.

7. H. Schürmann, *Das Lukasevangelium* (Freiburg, 1969), p. 325.

8. The symbol // will be used to indicate synoptic parallels.

9. See, e.g., Schürmann, *Lukasevangelium,* p. 324.

10. This is the position of Degenhardt, *Lukas,* pp. 39, 44, etc.

11. Hans Conzelmann, *The Theology of St. Luke,* trans. Geoffrey Buswell (New York: Harper & Row, p. 1961), p. 233, is correct in saying that the poverty of the disciples is something now past, but he does not allow for its relevance in principle to Luke and his community: "One *can* still be required to leave all" (italics added); "Luke's

ethical thinking is determined not by 'imitatio' but by discipleship, in a form appropriate to the particular time." For criticism of the salvation-historical "schema" that Conzelmann assumes for Luke's dual work, see C. Burchard, *Der dreizehnte Zeuge* (Göttingen, 1970).

12. In this connection Lk. 5:32 shows clearly that Luke makes deliberate grammatical alterations. Here he has the perfect tense, because the coming of Jesus still perdures, whereas Mk. 2:17 uses the aorist.

13. For the interpretation of this verse in Luke, see above, chap.1.III.5.

14. See, e.g., Conzelmann, *Theology of St. Luke*, pp. 233ff., and more recently W. Schmithals, "Lukas, Evangelist der Armen," *Theologia Viatorum* 12 (1973–74): 153–67.

15. Luke 18:35–43—the healing of a blind beggar—is not a story about a disciple. It is said indeed that after being cured the blind man "followed" Jesus (v. 43); but this following was a response to the healing and not a following specifically as a disciple.

16. See above, chapter 2. I 3, excursus.

17. See H. Hommel, "Das hellenistische Ideal vom einfachen Leben," *Studium Generale* 11 (1958): 742–51, and R. Vischer, *Das einfache Leben* (Göttingen, 1965), on the ideal of the simple life in Greek and Roman literature.

18. The warning that one should test oneself carefully before embarking on a difficult undertaking is also found in Epictetus, *Discourses* III, 22.

19. Luke differs here from the Socratic tradition; see H. Hommel, "Herrenworte im Lichte sokratischer Uberlieferung," *ZNTW* 57 (1966):1–23.

20. Epictetus, *Discourses* III, 22.

21. Ibid., trans. P. E. Matheson, in W. J. Oates, ed., *The Stoic and Epicurean Philosophers* (New York: Random House, 1940), p. 382.

22. Ibid., (trans. Matheson, p. 380).

23. Diogenes Laertius VI, 87f. (trans. R. D. Hicks, in Loeb Classics [Cambridge, Mass.: Harvard Univ. Press, 1959], vol. 2, pp. 91–93).

24. Lucian, *De morte Peregrini.*

25. Cf. Lk. 5:11, 28; 14:26; 18:29; 9:1–6, 23–27, 51–62; 10:1–16.

26. On this, see Helm, "Kynismus," in Pauly-Wissowa 23:3–24.

27. Lucian, *Cynicus* 6–8 (trans. M. D. Macleod, in *Lucian,* vol. 8 [Loeb Classics, Cambridge, Mass.: Harvard Univ. Press, 1969]).

28. On the interpretation of this story in the earliest tradition, see above, chap. 1.IV.

29. On the parable of the lost son, see Luise Schottroff, "Das Gleichnis vom verlorenen Sohn," *ZTK* 68 (1971): 27ff.

30. H. Hommel, "Menanders *Dyskolos*—Schmuck und Flicken am Gewand des Misanthropen," in *Festschrift zum 65: Geburtstag von W. Mönch* (Heidelberg, 1971), pp. 13–68.

31. See the material in G. Delling, "Pleonektēs," *TDNT* 6:266ff.

32. Plutarch, *De cupiditate divitiarum* 7.

33. On the prices of grain and their importance in antiquity, see Prov. 11:26. In Cicero, *Verrine* II, 3, 227, we find the statement: "The price of grain is high only when a crop fails; if the harvest is rich, the price goes down."

34. In connection with Lk. 12:21, see also Philo, *De specialibus legibus* IV, 73.

35. On this problem at the level of the Sayings-source, see above, chap. 2.III.1.

36. Joachim Jeremias, *The Parables of Jesus,* trans. S. H. Hooke (rev. ed.; New York: Scribner, 1963), p. 177.

37. Pliny, *Epistulae* IX, 37.

38. See L. Friedländer, *Darstellungen aus der Sittengeschichte Roms* (Leipzig, 1922), vol. 1, chap. 1, on social intercourse.

39. See Plato, *Crito* 53A.

40. Part of this dialogue, in Lucian's *Dialogues*, was quoted earlier, chap. 1. III.9.

41. Lucian, *Dialogues of the Dead* 1, no. 3 (quotations from Macleod translation, in *Lucian*, vol. 7 [Loeb Classics, Cambridge, Mass.: Harvard Univ. Press, 1961]).

42. See W. C. van Unnik, "Die Motivierung der Feindesliebe in Lukas VI, 32-35," *NovTest* 8 (1966): 234-300.

43. Pohlmann, *Geschichte der sozialen Frage*, vol. 2, p. 470.

44. For the parallels in Plato and Aristotle, see D. L. Mealand, "Community of Goods and Utopian Allusions in Acts II-IV," *JTS* 28 (1977): 96-99.

45. Iamblichus, *De vita Pythagorica* 30, 167f.

46. Cf. also Seneca, *Epistulae* 90, 38: "in which you cannot find a poor person."

47. This was shown recently by Martin Hengel, "Between Jesus and Paul: The 'Helenists,' the 'Seven' and Stephen (Acts 6: 1-15; 7: 54-83)," in his *Between Jesus and Paul: Studies in the Earliest History of Christianity,* trans. John Bowden (Philadelphia: Fortress Press, 1983), pp. 1-29.

48. On this, see U. Kahrstedt, *Kulturgeschichte der römischen Kaiserzeit* (Munich, 1944), pp. 45f., and elsewhere.

Index of Scriptural References

Compiled by James Sullivan

OLD TESTAMENT

NEW TESTAMENT